TELMORE

12.28

40 %

<

13. oktober 2017
16.43

Rediger

just tie knots

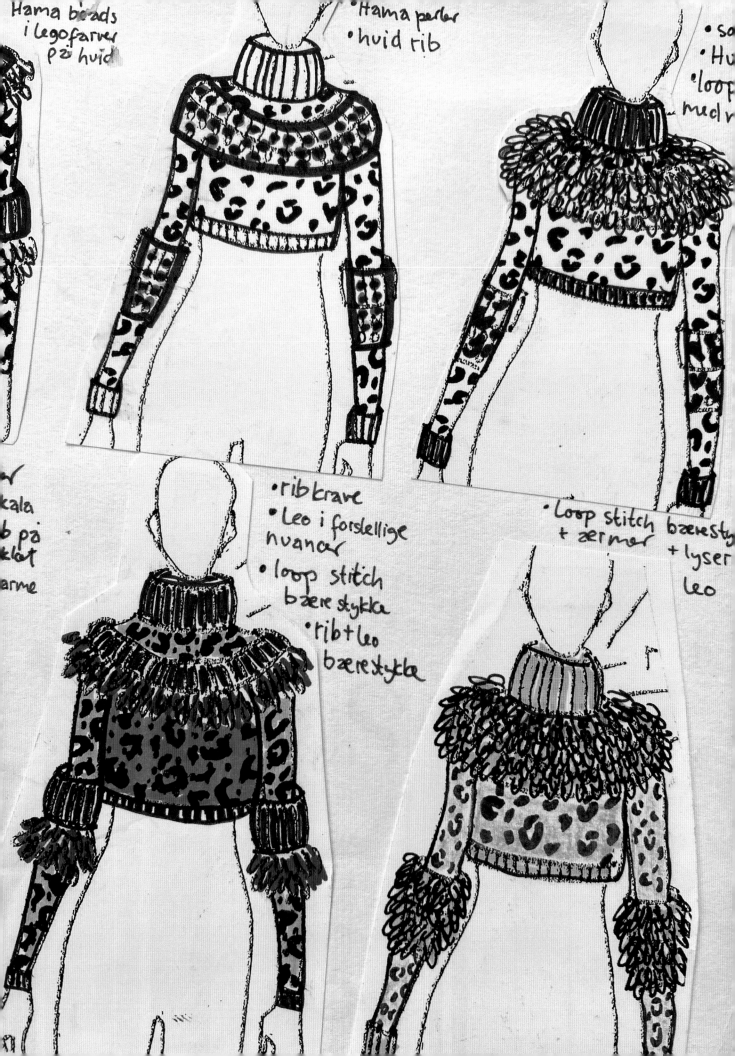

Hama beads
i legofarver
på hvid

•Hama perler
•hvid rib

•sa
•Hu
•loop
med r

•rib krave
•Leo i forskellige
nuancer
•loop stitch
bære stykke
•rib + leo
bærestykke

•Loop stitch bærestyk
+ ærmer
+ lyser
leo

kala
b på
klæt
arme

Lærke Bagger

close knit

15 Patterns and
45 Techniques from
Beginner to Advanced
from Europe's Coolest
Knitter

PRESTEL
Munich · London · New York

Cover design by Luisa Klose, using photos by Peter Stanners (front)
and Lærke Bagger (back).

The front cover shows a detail of the photo on p. 237. The basic
instructions for the loop pattern used here can be found on
p. 232ff. The instructions for this technique in one colour can
be found on p. 238 ff.
The version shown on the cover was made by creatively
combining different colours of yarn.

First published in Danish under the title *Lærke Bagger strik* by
Gyldendal Nonfiktion, Klareboderne 3, 1115 Copenhagen
© Lærke Bagger & Gyldendal, Copenhagen 2021
Published by agreement with Gyldendal Group Agency

For the English Edition
© Prestel Verlag, Munich · London · New York 2022
A member of Penguin Random House Verlagsgruppe GmbH
Neumarkter Strasse 28 · 81673 Munich

Library of Congress Control Number is available; a CIP catalogue
record for this book is available from the British Library.

Cover of the Danish edition and principal layout: Spine Studio
Graphic design completion: Nethe Ellinge
Editorial assistance Gyldendal: Mette Kofod Christensen
Illustrations: Klara Graah
Photos: Lærke Bagger, Peter Stanners, Sidsel Alling and
Fryd Frydendahl

Editorial direction Prestel: Claudia Stäuble
Project management: Andrea Bartelt-Gering
Translation from German: Jane Michael, Munich
Copy editing: Melanie Girdlestone for booklab GmbH, Munich
Production management: Luisa Klose
Typesetting: Katalin Golya, booklab GmbH, Munich

Printing and binding: Livonia Print, Riga

Penguin Random House Publishing Group FSC® N001967

MIX
Paper from responsible sources
FSC® C002795

Printed in Latvia

ISBN 978-3-7913-8886-1
www.prestel.com

A bit about knit-shaming and insecurity, and — what the hell! — a LOT about knitting.

There were just three things I really cared about before I had children: knitting, parties and cool clothes. In that order, please note.

Since childhood, crafts have been a constant in my life, and I always dreamed of making my own clothes. But I didn't really like sewing and was too impatient to design things, as you have to produce numerous versions of a particular style before it is finally perfect. I wanted instant fun, so I picked up some needles and yarn and got started. But at the same time, I wanted to party and finish quickly so I could throw a bash in my cool new pullover. I've always been someone who could enjoy life to the full, and so knitting became my world.

It might sound easy to just start knitting, but it really wasn't – believe me. I would be a millionaire by now if I'd got a euro every time someone said, "You'll never make a living with that" or "Bad idea. Forget it". But all I wanted to do was knit. I just had to seize the opportunity and put all my eggs in one basket, no matter what the result would be.

This guy once described me as a totally pathetic "Knitty Nora". And he wasn't joking. He made the comment to hurt me. I was young and sensitive and had plucked up the courage for the first time to express out loud my dream of making a living from my knitting. At first, I was really upset. The words pathetic Knitty Nora gave me stomach cramps, quite apart from the insecurity and fear I was feeling anyway. Was I really so bad? Was he right, perhaps, and my dream was as impossible as it was stupid?

No, dammit! Gradually his words became more than ridicule and mockery to me. They became a statement I simply had to prove wrong, come what may. I wanted to prove – to myself, not to him – that I was not a totally untalented Knitty Nora. His words became a mantra that made me defiant. They were more important for my career than all the times I heard the words "well done!" It's crazy, I know.

This book is about finding the courage to stand your ground and use insecurity as a driving force. CLOSE KNIT is much more than just a knitting manual. It's about believing in yourself, not caring what others think and not wanting to be perfect and neat but having fun and accepting the mistakes you make when you enter unknown territory.

Oh boy, have I made mistakes! And I still make them now – every day. I was never the most talented, the best, the prettiest or the Number One in anything. Believe me. But I was prepared to apply myself and tackle the seemingly impossible and uncertain. In short, I was banking on success.

This book is another project like that. I have dreamed of producing it for over ten years but have never actually dared to publish it. And I can't remember ever having shed as many tears as I did over the work on this book. It was hard, really tough – but awesome fun and great for me.

So, knitting. Obviously, CLOSE KNIT is about knitting, but it's not a typical knitting manual – because I'm not your typical knitter. Nor a knitting expert. I'm just an expert in being Lærke Bagger and knitting the way Lærke Bagger knits. So this book contains my thoughts, techniques, tips and my own abbreviations – and of course 15 of my designs.

CLOSE KNIT is a book for novices as well as dyed-in-the wool knitters. You can read it from start to finish or use it as a reference book. The 15 patterns increase in difficulty, so you can improve your techniques step by step. So, even if you have an advanced degree in knitting and can probably knit better than me, you might still find a few useful tips here and there. My designs aren't that easy, so you might find them as hard to knit as this book was for me to write – because I don't have any precise instructions for techniques, colours and patterns.

But what CLOSE KNIT does have is plenty of suggestions and guidelines that will require you to take decisions and experiment yourself – so you also need the courage to make mistakes, because the mistakes are part of the design. In other words, they aren't really mistakes at all, because my designs are personal rather than perfect. Nothing is more boring than perfection. Our mistakes are the best things about us. They are what make us human.

My aim with this book was to create a framework for you to develop your own ideas. So you can vary all 15 designs in countless ways: with the various Scrap techniques, beads, in a single colour with embroidered stitches, or all of the above.

Create your own universe, based on your own aesthetics, preferences, yarn and abilities. In short, adapt all the instructions in this book as you like, to suit yourself. Take the techniques as suggestions you can combine. There's no right or wrong in knitting.

I want this book to inspire you, make you want to face challenges and try out something new. If you're interested in seeing how other people knit my designs, check out social media and the hashtags for my designs. It's incredible to see the variety and how different my designs look when they come from someone else's needles.

There's an absolutely fantastic knitting community on social media that offers encouragement and networks across all ages and nationalities. Let's keep on inspiring each other.

Carpe diem!

All the best, Lærke Bagger

Chapter 1
Knitting Techniques (the easy ones)

"It's basic stuff. Just go for it. Have no fear. And a bit about the knitting equipment you need."

CASTING ON

Just do it! Are you new to knitting? Finding it daunting? Have no fear. Just give it a whirl. You can always chuck it and start again. But don't just bin it: cut the yarn, unravel it and use it again.

The first thing you need is knitting needles and yarn. If this is your first time, use a light-coloured yarn. That way, it's easier to see what you're doing when you cast on.

There are various techniques for casting on. I use the long-tail method because that's the one my mother taught me. None of my designs actually requires long-tail casting on, so just use whatever method you like best. Some people like to use two needles or a larger size than the needles they'll be using for the main knitting. I prefer to use the same size needle because it makes a nice, firm edge. If you tend to knit fairly tightly, you can cast on with needles one size larger than what's listed in the knitting pattern. Showing someone via a book how cast on in a way that's easy to follow and to understand is almost impossible, so I suggest you search the Web or ask someone you know to show you.

You can also use two threads for the long-tail cast-on method: a basic thread (p. 96) and a scrap thread (p. 97). Don't worry about knots in the cast-on edge. They look great and will give your knitting character.

PRACTISE!

- Practise casting on with needles of various sizes. It'll give you a feel for the firmness of your knitting, and at the same time you will be practising the sequence of steps.

- Also, practise casting on with different yarns and with numbers of threads. You'll notice that it makes a huge difference whether you're knitting with cotton or wool.

KNIT STITCH

Knit stitch - also known as 'plain knitting' – is abbreviated. It's the easiest stitch to do and a good way to practise. It's a basic knitting technique.

There are various ways to do knit stitch. The two most common are the continental and the American/English methods. The main difference lies in which hand you use to hold the yarn. In the American/English method, you hold the yarn in your right hand and wind it around the needle; in the continental method you hold it with your left and lift it over the needle.

The Not So Heavy Sweater (p. 178) is knitted entirely in knit stitch (or 'plain knitting'). The result is called 'garter stitch'. Here it is knitted using the ATS Scrap technique (p. 102). Looks awesome!

Knit stitch (continental method)

1 Hold the yarn behind your work, in your left hand, draped over your extended index finger. Hold the needle with the cast-on stitches in your left hand and the empty needle in your right hand. Insert the right-hand needle into the front loop of the first stitch on the left-hand needle.

2 Loop the yarn round the tip of the needle by sliding the right-hand needle behind the yarn.

3 Pull the yarn, which is now lying across the right-hand needle, forwards through the stitch on the left-hand needle.

4 Slip the stitch you have just knitted from the left-hand needle onto the right-hand needle. You did it!

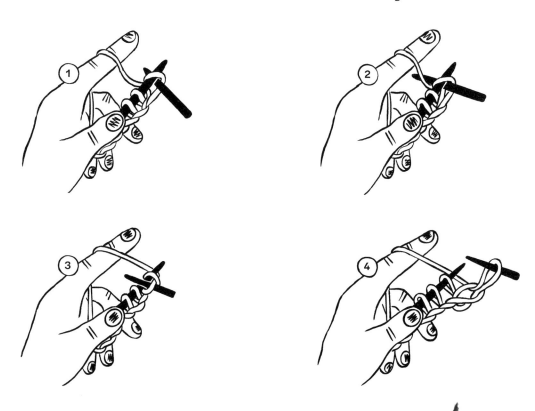

Do the same with all the stitches on the left needle. When you're done, all the stitches will be on your right needle – and hey presto! You've knitted a row! Now swap the needles over so you're holding the needle with all the stitches in your left hand again. Do your next row of plain knitting stitches by following the five steps described above. If you continue knitting back and forth like this, you'll produce a pattern called garter stitch, or plain knitting. It's a lovely stitch that looks the same on both sides – see the patterns on pages 138, 146 and 179.

Knit stitch (English/American method)

1 Hold the yarn behind your work, in your right hand. Hold the needle with the cast-on stitches in your left hand. Insert the tip of the right needle into the front of loop of the first stitch on the left one.

2 With your right hand, slip the yarn between the needles, looping it from left to right.

3 Keep the yarn fairly tight over the right-hand needle and start to pull it through the stitch using the tip of your right needle.

4 Pull the right needle and yarn right through the stitch to form a new stitch on your right needle.

5 Slip the loop off the left needle and your first new stitch is done! It is now on your right needle. Fantastic!

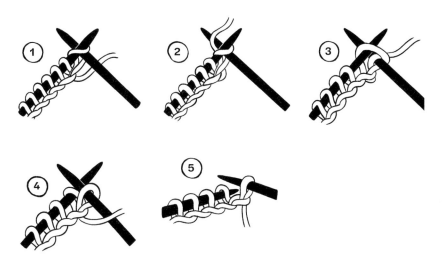

PURL STITCH

Purl is abbreviated p. This is a little harder than knit stitch but not really too much bother. There are lots of different ways of knitting purl, so I'm going to tell you my favourite. If your mum, friend, uncle, dad or someone on YouTube tells you another way that you find better, then use that.

On page 33 you'll see a garment made of flat, almost woven-looking stitches. This is the effect you get when you alternate between a row of knit ('plain') stitches and a row of purl stitches. It's called stocking stitch.

A lot of people hate purl – which I think is a pity. But I've always had a soft spot for underdogs, so I LOOOVE doing purl. Life has its ups and downs, and so does knitting. Purl takes a bit more patience and can be a bit irritating until you get the knack. But it does make you appreciate knit stitch all the more!

Best, Your kitchen-table *philosopher* Lærke

Purl stitch (continental method)

1 Hold the yarn in front of your work, in your left hand, draped over your extended index finger. Hold the needle with the cast-on stitches in your left hand and the empty needle in your right hand. Insert the right-hand needle from the right into the front loop of the first stitch on the left-hand needle.

2 Lay the right-hand needle behind the yarn and wind the yarn round the needle from front to back. Now you have a loop round the needle.

3 Pull the loop on the right-hand needle through the loop on the left-hand needle.

4 Slip the stitch you have just knitted from the left-hand needle onto the right-hand needle. You did it again! Purl all the stitches on the left-hand needle. When all the stitches are on the right-hand needle, turn your work and knit another row. (If you are doing stocking stitch, your next row will be in knit stitch.)

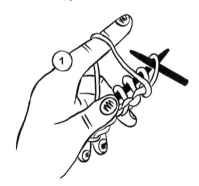
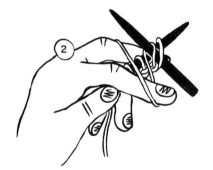
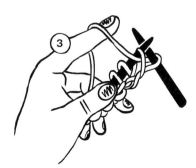
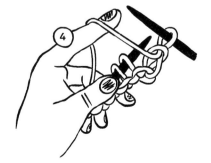

Purl stitch (English/American method)

1 Hold the yarn in front of your work, in your right hand. Hold the needle with the cast-on stitches in your left hand. Insert the tip of the right needle through your first stitch from right to left.

2 Wind the yarn from right to left over the right-hand needle.

3 Keep the yarn fairly tight over the right needle and start to pull the needle back through the stitch on the left needle.

4 Pull the right needle and yarn right through the stitch to form a new stitch on your right needle.

5 Slip the original stitch off the left needle and you're done. The new stitch is now on your right needle. Fantastic!.

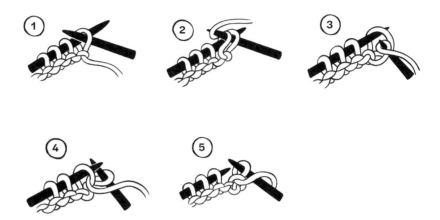

THE RIB EDGE: PLAIN KNITTING INTO THE BACK OF THE STITCH

The Cute Top (p. 208), knitted using the Bad Idea Scrap technique (p. 110).

- To knit into the back loop of the stitch (k1tbl), insert the right needle into the loop of the stitch behind the needle. Then proceed as described on p. 24–25. A LOT of my beaded pullovers and edges use this method.

Wrong side of The Cute Top (p. 208), knitted using the Bad Idea Scrap technique (p. 110).

<

Wrong side of The Bad Idea Top (p. 226). The basic colours (p. 110) are lime and pink, my two favourite colours.

>

PURL STITCH INTO THE BACK OF THE STITCH FOR POLO NECKS

- You can purl into the back of the stitch for polo necks. I don't do this very often, but I always use it for long roll necks (pp. 166 and 172) and sometimes for beaded pullovers (p. 252). Insert the right-hand needle from behind, through the back loop of the stitch instead of through the front.

29

Garter-stitch stripes in different yarns will produce The Bad Idea Blanket (p. 138) – or a great scarf.

GARTER STITCH

I love garter stitch. It basically consists of plain knitting for every row. It creates a lovely *old-school* feel, like a summer cottage. If you're not very experienced and don't knit tight, it can be quite hard to get garter stitch to look even. So I suggest using needles a size or two smaller than the pattern states. Garter stitch is the easiest way to knit. Both sides look the same, the edge doesn't curl up, and it looks great!

If you want to knit garter stitch on a circular needle, you will need to do a round of purl followed by a round of plain. I found it quite easy to knit garter stitch on a round needle. I knitted the Original Bad Idea Dress on a circular needle, with 420 stitches and alternate rows of knit and purl.

PRACTISE!

- Knit garter stitch with different types of yarn – together or separately. That way you will get a feel for how firm or loose your knitting is. Try out different sizes of needle, as this can make all the difference between it looking fantastic or dreadful! Combine different types and colours of yarn that might not appear to go together at first. You might end up with something surprisingly attractive. And it's great fun, too!

The crazy Bad Idea Dress that eventually turned out great. And my daughter Lulu. You will find a similar pattern using garter stitch on page 226.

Stocking stitch
knitted with different
needle sizes, yarns
and colours.

STOCKING STITCH

I reckon stocking stitch is the most frequently used knitting stitch and the basis of almost all knitting. It consists of alternate rows of plain and purl stitches. If you're using a circular needle, you'll achieve the same effect just by doing every round in plain.

Normally the smooth side of your stocking stitch will be the outside of your garment. But I really like the other side (the "purl" side) as well. You can basically knit almost all the designs in this book "inside-out", with the smooth side on the inside and the "purl" side on the outside, if you like. If you want to use the "purl" side on the outside, knit your pullover according to the pattern but make sure you leave your yarn ends on the "smooth" side. And if you have to sew in ends or pick up stitches around the neck edge, turn your knitting round and do it with the smooth side facing you. So, if you want to use the "purl" side as the outside of the garment, you will need to do everything the other way round.

Here's how to count rows and stitches for garter stitch and stocking stitch. It's really useful if you've forgotten where you are in the pattern – which happens to me constantly!

How to count rows and stitches

1   In stocking stitch, the stitches are v-shaped. Each v is one stitch.

2   In garter stitch, the stitches are wave-shaped. Each wave is one stitch.

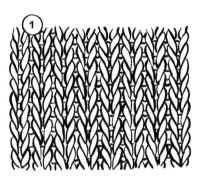
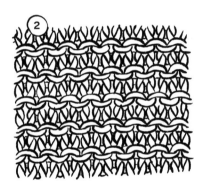

PRACTISE!

- Change colours, combine different types of yarn, knit stripes, and change yarn or colour in the middle or at the edge. Off you go!

33

Wide rib pattern for The Easy Peasy Pillow (p. 132). If you knit with thick needles, it will look fabulous, with a great 3D effect.

Rib in moss stitch on The Lulu Sweater Dress (p. 158). Knitted in stripes using the All Over Scrap technique (p. 106).

RIB PATTERNS

A rib pattern consists of a combination of knit and purl stitches knitted alternately in rows or rounds. It's often used for cuffs, neckbands, waistbands and items requiring structure or elasticity. There are countless rib patterns, such as 1/1 (k1, p1) or 2/2 (k2, p2). If you knit your rib pattern back and forth on straight needles, you will knit the "odd" rows the other way round, with a purl stitch directly above a knit stitch, and vice versa. A 1/1 rib pattern goes like this:

1st row: k1, p1, repeat to end of row
2nd row: k1, p1, repeat to end of row

Moss stitch is another variant of the rib pattern and goes like this:

1st row: k1, p1, repeat to end of row
2nd row: p1, k1, repeat to end of row

For either of the above, you will need **an even number of stitches**.

Thin mohair knitted with a thicker basic yarn to make The Bad Idea Top (p. 226). Also looks awesome!

MY GO-TO RIB PATTERN

- I mostly use a 1/1 rib pattern, which I create by knitting into the backs of the stitches (p. 26). This gives it a nice 3D look and a more clearly defined stitch pattern. It's very easy to do. Here's how:

  1st row: k1tbl (through back of loop, p1, repeat to end of row.
  2nd row: k1, p1tbl (through back of loop), repeat to end of row.
  Don't forget to use an even number of stitches!

PRACTISE!

- Experiment with different rib patterns. For example:

  1/1 rib (with an even number of stitches)
  1st row: k1, p1, repeat to end of row
  2nd row: p1, k1, repeat to end of row

  2/2 rib (number of stitches must be a multiple of four)
  1st row: k2, p2, repeat to end of row
  2nd row: p2, k2, repeat to end of row

- If you change over in the middle of the rib pattern and have a purl above a knit (and vice versa), you'll produce checks instead of ribs. You can knit an incredible number of textured patterns using just these two basic stitch types.

EDGE STITCHES (alias BUTT stitches)

The edge stitches are the stitches at each end of your knitting. I'm dogmatic when it comes to edge stitches, and I only ever use one type: BUTT stitches (as I like to call them!). I learned this technique from my grandma, who also taught me how important neat edges are for stitching a garment together. But it wasn't grandma who called edge stitches *butts*! I assume she called them something different. But personally, I think edge stitches look like a butt and can't remember the real name for them anyway – sorry, Granny. There are lots of methods for dealing with edge stitches. This is mine. If you prefer a different one, use that.

The BUTT

1   Your yarn comes out of the first stitch on your left needle. Pull it backwards and upwards in front of the needle and you'll see the loops of the stitch look like two thighs.

2   Insert the right needle through the stitch from the back and lift off the without knitting it. This twists the BUTT so it will end up on the outer edge.

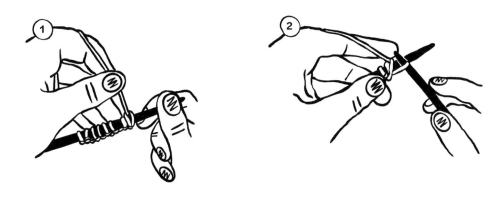

The illustrations show the technique with the yarn held according to the continental method, see p. 24.

Knit, knit, knit, until there's just one stitch remaining on your left needle, then k1 the last stitch. Do this on every row. I repeat: plain-knit the last stitch in every row, regardless of the pattern. That way, both edges of your work look the same. Repeat these edge stitches at the beginning and end of every row. I call the two threads that form the edge stitches "loops" or "legs".

The BUTT edge basically consists of just two different stitches, regardless of whether you are doing garter stitch, stocking stitch, rib or moss stitch: the BUTT stitch at the beginning of each row and the knit stitch at the end of each row.

STRAIGHT, CIRCULAR AND DOUBLE-POINTED NEEDLES – AND OTHER KNITTING ACCESSORIES

You can knit on straight knitting needles, so-called cardigan needles, circular needles or double-pointed needles. The thickness of needles is measured in millimetres (continental system). The U.S. has its own numbering system, and the UK now uses the continental system, although old patterns may still use the old English system. Conversion charts are available. So, when should you use which needles?

When you knit back and forth, you knit all the stitches from one needle to the other and then turn the work round and do the same again. First one needle and then the other. This is how to knit with straight ('cardigan') knitting needles.

Double-pointed needles are best for small, circular items like socks or sleeves, or as extra needles for techniques that need more than two knitting needles, such as pleats (p. 224).

Circular needles are mostly used for knitting larger circular. But they're also great for knitting back and forth as you would with normal straight needles, for instance if you have a lot of stitches in a row. It can be difficult to cram large numbers of stitches onto a straight needle.

And yes, circular needles come in various lengths. The short ones are for necklines and sleeves, the long ones for round yokes and shawls etc. I've never taken much notice of the length, but I don't like the very short ones (40 cm) because they are difficult to hold. And very long ones (over 80 cm) tend to get twisted. So I usually knit on a circular needle that's 60 cm or 80 cm long, but mostly it is pure chance which one I use. I just use whatever happens to be lying on the table.

Circular needles with exchangeable cables are great, but normal ones are fine as well! I use both kinds.

PRACTISE!

- With circular needles, you just keep knitting round and round. You cast on using the circular needle, join the two ends of the circular needle together and then knit the stitches from the left needle onto the right one. When you bring the two ends of the needle together to join them up, make sure your cast-on stitches are all below the needle, not twisted around it. Otherwise, you'll find that – depressing as it may be – after a few rounds of knitting, you have to unravel the whole thing. It happens to the best of us and will probably happen to you some day too!

Sleeves for The Carpe Diem Sweater (p. 252), knitted on double-pointed needles using the Bad Idea Scrap technique.

Circular needle for The Bad Idea Top (p. 226), row with pleat (p. 224).

HOW TO CHOOSE YOUR KNITTING NEEDLES

- **Knit with different sizes of needle:** If you're doing stocking stitch and there are irregular stripes on the front, you're almost certainly knitting the purl rows more loosely than the knit rows. Try knitting the knit rows on a thicker needle. That means you will be knitting with two different needle sizes.

- **Interchangeable needle tips:** If you're knitting back and forth on a circular needle with interchangeable tips (p. 39) and find your purl rows are looser than your knit ones, try changing one of the needles. Use a thicker needle for the knit rows and a thinner one for the purl rows.

- **Double-pointed needles:** For sleeves, socks or other small circular items, it's best to use double-pointed needles or the Magic Loop technique (p. 41). Some people find knitting with four needles irritating because you have to hold your work differently. But I like a lot. It makes me feel like a real knitter.

Casting on with ordinary knitting needles for The Easy Peasy Pillow (p. 132).

MAGIC LOOP

The *Magic Loop* method allows you to knit circular items with just a few stitches on circular needles and means you don't need double-pointed needles. It's not a special tool but a technique that's often used for sleeves, socks and hats – for smallish items with not many stitches in each row. Whether you prefer to work with double-pointed needles or the *Magic Loop* is up to you. Personally, I've never quite decided which I prefer. Sometimes I use double-pointed needles for cuffs or socks, and sometimes I use the Magic Loop for sleeves knitted in stocking stich. It is virtually impossible to explain the *Magic Loop* technique in a book, so please use the internet – not because it's particularly complicated but because it requires a long sequence of manoeuvres that are impossible to describe in an easy-to-understand way.

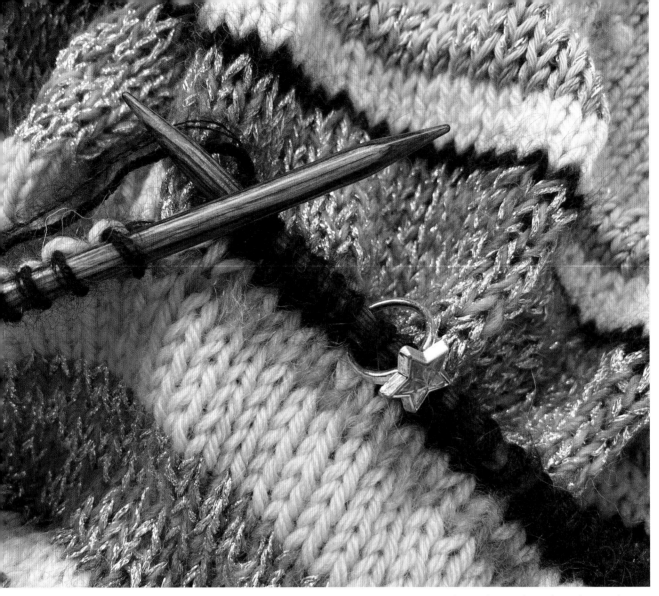

Rings also make good stitch markers. Lulu was kind enough to lend me some of her prettiest ones.

STITCH MARKERS

You can use stitch markers to mark things like the beginning of a round, a side of a pullover, or a seam. There's a huge variety of attractive and expensive markers on the market, and I like them a lot – but I'm forever losing them! So I tend to just take a short length of yarn and knot it into a loop to slip over the stitch. I also use rubber bands, paper clips or whatever else I have available (see above). I use one colour to mark the beginning of the round and another to mark the edge or seam. That way I don't get confused and decrease when I shouldn't. To mark the beginning of a round, slip the marker onto the knitting needle and carry on knitting. When you get back to the marker, you'll know you're back at the beginning again. Slip the marker from the left needle to the right one and keep knitting.

Make your own markers and mark, for example, every 20th cast-on stitch. That way you won't need to keep re-counting every stitch.

AVOID ETERNAL STITCH-COUNTING

- If you've cast on a large number of stitches, for example for The Bad Idea Top (p. 226) or The Lulu Sweater Dress (p. 158), I have a fantastic tip from my supercool mother-in-law, so you don't have to keep re-counting your stitches:

- When you cast on, place a marker on your needle after every 20 or 50 stitches. That way you won't have to keep counting from the beginning. You can just add up the stitches using the markers while you are knitting the first round or row. Thank you so much, Mother-in-Law! If only I'd known that when I was knitting The Bad Idea Dress! I recommend this method if you've cast on more than 200 stitches.

43

KNITTING TENSION AND TENSION SQUARES

Tension checks for The Not So Heavy Sweater (p. 178). Honestly, this pull-over is so cool!

Knitting tension? What on earth is that? Why does it matter? And why does it sometimes not matter? How do we measure it? This is important: your knitting tension determines how many stitches you have to knit for, say, 10 cm of knitting – which in turn depends on how firmly or loosely you knit. You can check by knitting a tension square, which is a 10 x 10 cm square made with the recommended yarn on the recommended needles in the recommended pattern according to the instructions you are following. Your knitting tension must correspond with what it says in the pattern – the same number of stitches wide and the same number of rows high – otherwise your garment won't have the measurements it says in the pattern. What you'd intended as size L could come out as an S.

If the tension square is the wrong size, use needles a size larger or smaller to knit another test square and see if it is now the correct size. It's a bit annoying, I know! By the way, make sure your hands are relaxed as you knit your tensions square so as not to knit tighter or looser than normal. Otherwise, your tension square will give you the wrong result. You must knit it as you would if you were sitting on the sofa watching reality TV – because when you watch the telly, you won't sit there remembering to knit tighter or looser. Instead, you'll simply knit away. So in that case, if your tension square doesn't match what the knitting pattern says, try another needle size and knit a new one. Keep doing that until you get the right size.

There are all sorts of cool gadgets for measuring your knitting tension, but an easy way is to cut a square hole measuring 10 x 10 cm in a piece of card and lay the card on your knitting (p. 45). Then count the number of stitches and rows you can see in the cut-out window. Count horizontally as well as vertically. The number of stitches counting horizontally gives your knitting tension in the width, e.g. 11 stitches for 10 cm across. The number of rows counting vertically is your knitting tension in the height, e.g. 17 rows for 10 cm up. So in that case, your tension square is 11 stitches x 17 rows for 10 x 10 cm. It's best to you count in several places and calculate the average of your measurements.

During the first ten years that I was knitting, I never made a tension square. Ever! Even now, I only do it because I have to. It's important for me as a designer so I can provide completely accurate information about lengths and widths. But quite honestly, it really is boring to have to knit something so stupid before you can get started on the fantastic pullover want to wear next Friday. That's why I never used to bother – which makes me a real hypocrite, telling you to do one every time! But there is absolutely no doubt about it: you can't achieve the best result without a tension square. So my official advice is: always knit a tension square!

I will admit, however, that I really love the element of risk if you don't do one. I'm one of those *ride-or-die people* who finds a certain charm in refusing to take control and plan.

Oh yes, and I never treat and wash my tension squares, but that's a matter of taste. On page 262 you'll find everything you need to know about treating and washing things. But you must be consistent. So if you treat your tension square, you'll have to do the same with your knitted garment.

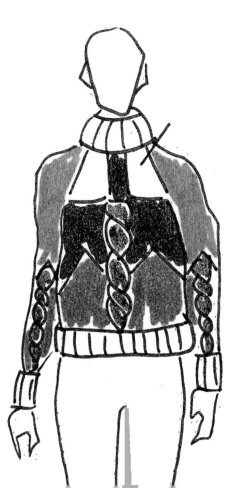

SAVE YOUR TENSION SQUARES

- We often choose the same yarn types again and again, so if you save your tension squares you won't need to knit another one the next time you have the same yarn and needles. But do remember to label each square with information about the tension, yarn, colour number and needle size. Even if you think you'll remember, you can be sure you'll have forgotten just when you really need it!

CASTING OFF AND FINISHING

Casting off means finishing off a piece of knitting, either completely or in part. How cool is that? It means you've finished all or part of your garment. Congratulations! There are lots of different ways of casting off, but I prefer the easiest one, so I mostly cast off with plain knitting. I like the firmness and simplicity of its no-fuss appearance.

Casting off in five steps

1 Knit the first two stitches onto the right-hand needle.

2 Insert the tip of the left needle into the first of the stitches on the right-hand needle. To do this, approach it from the left.

3 Pull it over the second stitch you knitted and let it slip off and under the needle. That stitch has now been cast off.

4 Knit the next stitch so you have two stitches on the right needle again. Pull the first stitch over the second one as in step 3. Keep going in the same way until there's just one stitch left on your right needle.

5 Cut the yarn, leaving a length of about 15-20 cm. You will need this extra length to stitch the garment together or to knot the yarn. Pull the yarn through the last stitch and give it a good tug.

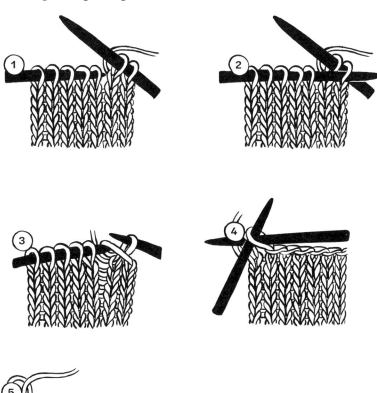

The Easy Peasy Pillow (p. 132).
Knitted in stocking stitch using the
All Over Scrap technique (p. 106).

Sometimes I cast off in rib, knitting over a knit and purling over a purl. Sounds tricky, but it isn't. Casting off in rib makes the neck edge more elastic. Cast off a knit stitch when the stitch below was also a knit, and cast off a purl if the stitch below was purl too.

Well, maybe you are thinking: "Okay, but what about casting off Italian style?" To be honest, I've never tried it because I'm too lazy and have two small kids. People say it's a great method, but I've never tried it out myself.

ASSEMBLING THE GARMENT

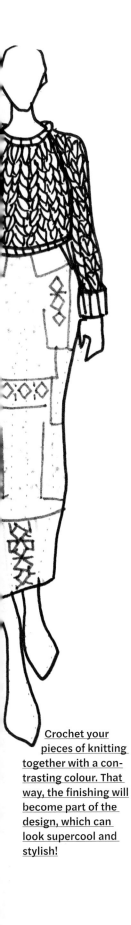

I find the best way of joining the pieces together is to crochet them. Full stop. If you have already tried it, you'll know what I mean. If not, get ready because your life will never be the same again. Crocheting pieces together is better than an awesome new handbag or pair of shoes, better than chips when you've got a hangover, better than sleep when you have a baby that won't – okay, maybe not, because then there really is nothing better than sleep.

Crocheting seams is incredibly easy and makes everything look classy, smart and perfect. And it's also very practical. But you need nice firm edges to do it – a BUTT edge (p. 37), for example. I learned how to do it when I was an intern at Sibling in London. My boss, Sid, was a brilliant knitwear designer who knew all the tricks. I was supposed to attach a collar to the back of a pullover, and when he saw me fiddling around with needle and thread, he started laughing and said, *"Oh my god, darling! What are you doing?"* He then showed me how to join the pieces with a crochet hook and slip stitch – and I've never used another method since.
    You can use this technique for everything: side seams, sleeve seams, shoulder seams, collars, closing armholes, attaching pockets, attaching cuffs, etc.

The trick is that you need a *steady hand*. Not too tight and not too loose, in other words. Fortunately, you can unpick crocheted seams, so if it goes wrong, you can simply try again. Use a crochet hook that's one or two sizes smaller than the knitting needles you used. But the size of the crochet needle doesn't matter too much, as long as you keep your crochet stitches a consistent length and tension.

Crocheting along a BUTT edge

This technique is incredibly easy. You just join the pieces with slip stitch. Unless otherwise instructed, always crochet with the right side (i.e. the outside) of your work facing you. I normally insert the hook through just one "cheek" (haha) of the BUTT stitch (one loop, in other words). If you insert it through both, the seam will be too thick. Sometimes I use the front loop and sometimes the back one. It depends on the design and function, but the pattern tells you how to do it best. I never sew my knitted pieces together, so there's no need ever to be afraid of knitting again for fear of sewing the pieces together. With this technique, the finishing is really fun.

Crochet your pieces of knitting together with a contrasting colour. That way, the finishing will become part of the design, which can look supercool and stylish!

49

Crocheting pieces together in three steps

1   Position the two knitted pieces you want to join so that their edges abut. Make sure the right sides facing you. Then decide whether you'll use the outer or the inner loop of the edge stitch to work with – and stick with your decision. Insert your crochet hook through your chosen (inner/outer) loop on one edge and then through the same chosen loop on the other. Lay the yarn across the crochet hook and pull it back through both loops.

2   Repeat this with the chosen loops of the next pair of edge stitches. You now have two loops on your crochet hook. Without laying the yarn across, pull the second loop through the first one so you have just one loop on the hook again. You have now joined the edges and cast off the first stitch – all at the same time. It looks fantastic!

3   Insert the crochet hook through the next loops of your knitting and continue as described in Step Two until you have joined the pieces as required.

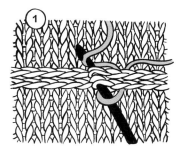 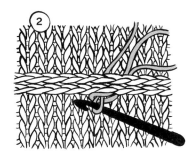 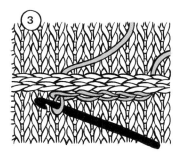

Make sure you don't pull the yarn too tight, otherwise the seam will pucker. And don't crochet too loosely either, otherwise the slip stitch will look irregular and ugly. This crochet method is basically the same as the one used industrially to join knitting pieces together. It's called a whipped seam.

If you need to slip-stitch round a square corner – for example on a blanket (p. 138) or a neckline (p. 56) – just crochet two or three loops into the same stitch. This will make the edge elastic. Follow your instinct as to how many loops you actually need and experiment a bit to see what looks best.

PRACTISE!

- Crochet various pieces of knitting together. It could be the side seams of a pullover or tension squares. And practise crocheting slip stitches with equal tension so they look regular.

The BUTT is also really great when you want a neat edge on something like The Larseman Cardigan (p.146). Simply slip-stitch through one or both loops on the edges. This will give you a nice firm edge that makes the whole garment look more harmonious.

Chapter 2
Knitting Techniques (the harder ones)

"Oh my god! Is she knitting from bottom to top? How to make the perfect neckline and why you should always measure yourself."

KNITTING FROM BOTTOM TO TOP

Here are the slightly more complicated techniques – in some ways, but not at all in others. They're based on what you already know. It might not sound that sexy, but boy will you feel sexy when you sit there with a perfectly executed neckline, I promise you. And I also have a few really important tips for finding the correct size.

Pullovers can be knitted from top to bottom, bottom to top or side to side. All the designs in this book are knitted from bottom to top. If you've never knitted that way before, don't worry – it's almost the same as knitting from top to bottom – just the other way round. If you want to adjust the length of a pullover, you just knit the front and back pieces longer or shorter than it says in the pattern. When you've knitted the back and front up to under the arms, stand in front of the mirror and see how the pullover falls around your hips and waist. We're all different shapes. My upper body is as long as my lower body, and my legs the length of a pizza pan.

In my knitting patterns the sleeves are also knitted from bottom to top. If you want the sleeves to be longer or shorter, check them regularly and cast off for the sleeve shaping when they're the right length. Later, when you assemble your garment, you will need to close these cast-off edges – which is easy to do with crocheted slip stitch (p. 58).

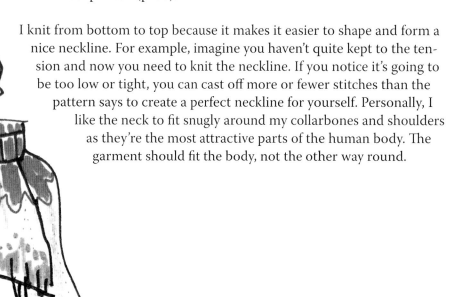

I knit from bottom to top because it makes it easier to shape and form a nice neckline. For example, imagine you haven't quite kept to the tension and now you need to knit the neckline. If you notice it's going to be too low or tight, you can cast off more or fewer stitches than the pattern says to create a perfect neckline for yourself. Personally, I like the neck to fit snugly around my collarbones and shoulders as they're the most attractive parts of the human body. The garment should fit the body, not the other way round.

Shit, I love nachos! The Bad Idea Top (p. 226), knitted using the Bad Idea Scrap technique (p. 110).

NECKLINES

The neckline is the icing on the cake. It's eye-catching and the first detail the eye rests on after a first impression. The neckline shows how skilful you are – or aren't. So it really is pretty important.

Until I was 27, there was something missing in my life as a knitter, although I couldn't quite put my finger on what it was. Every time I finished a pullover, I felt a lack of satisfaction, an emptiness. It never looked as good as on the pattern, and my necklines always looked awful. That was when I discovered the fold-in neckband I'd been missing all those years. A folded edge can make even truly untidy knitting look great.

I remember a meeting I once had in a nice shop in the centre of Copenhagen, early in my career. The owner wasn't entirely convinced of my talent and products until I told her that of course I'd started to create a new type of neckline, one that was much firmer and more attractive. Suddenly she was hooked. Necklines really are what makes the difference.

A neckband that would even impress your grandmother, in three steps

1   Knit the neckband in rib. Knit into the back of the knit stitches, and knit the purl stitches normally, unless otherwise instructed. That produces a firm, attractive appearance with straight, even rows.

2   Always pick up just one loop of the stitches around the edge of the neckline. If you pick up both, the seam will be too thick. It makes a slight difference whether you pick up the outer or the inner loop: if the garment you've knitted is very fluffy, fine or thin, pick up the inner loop to make it a bit firmer. If it's thick, pick up the outer loop so the seam doesn't turn out even thicker.

3   Make sure you cast off loosely around the neckline. The stitches need to be long enough to lie nicely around your neck and collarbones. You may have to unravel it a few times, but don't worry – I had to as well.

A nice neckline in four steps

1 Always pick up the stitches around the neckline with the right side of your work facing you. Start in the middle of the back. Over the years, I've discovered that the result always looks good if you pick up 9 stitches across every 10 stitches or rows. In other words, pick up 9 stitches and miss out the 10th stitch or row. I promise it will work. And you don't even have to count. Yay!

2 Knit the fold-over neckband until it is twice as long as the finished neckband needs to be.

3 Finish off with the wrong side of the work facing you. So, fold in the edge and turn the pullover inside out. Stitch or knot all yarn ends (p. 100). Start to crochet it down, working from the middle of the front, on the inside of the pullover. That way you won't have any thick bits/knots/ends in the nape of your neck that would be visible on your masterpiece, with its label stitched inside, when it's hanging on a hanger. All the ugly bits will be hidden away in the middle of the inside of the front.

4 Crochet the folded edge down using slip stitch (p. 49). To do this, pick up only one half of each stitch. Choose which half – either the outside or the inside loop – and stick to it. There's no need to crochet both loops. Insert the crochet hook into the loop of the cast-off edge and crochet it together with the first of the picked-up stitches in the same "column". What you see will look a bit like a ladder, in which you crochet the first "rung" into the last "rung". Carry on doing this all the way round.

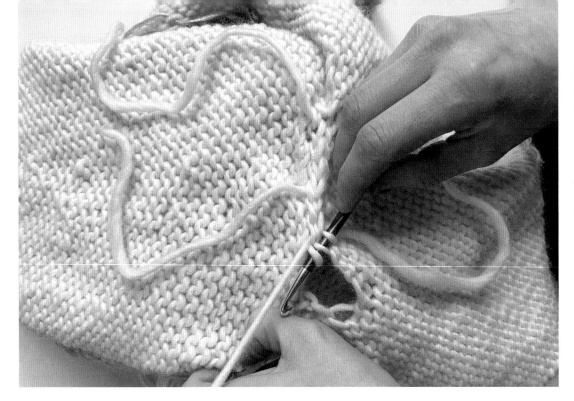

Closing armholes
with slip stitch
(p. 49).

<

Raglan armholes on
The Ombre Sweater
(p. 172), with a folded
neckband, knitted
in the basic colours
white and curry.

ARMHOLES

Underneath each sleeve is a short, flat, cast-off section. This gives your arms
room to move, and you'll need to crochet it closed to finish your garment.

When you've knitted the entire pullover, turn it inside out and crochet the gaps
together using slip stitch (p. 49). Put the cast-off armhole edges of the front and
back pieces facing the cast-off edge of the sleeve. Crochet them together from
right to left through the outer loops. Repeat for the other sleeve.

RAGLAN SLEEVES

There are various ways of shaping the silhouette of a pullover. Raglan sleeves
are my favourite. You can hardly go wrong with these as they have no seams
that relate directly to your body proportions – unless the shoulder seam of your
pullover is couple of centimetres away from your body, making you look like an
eight-year-old wearing their mum or dad's pullover. Also, raglan sleeves fit any
figure. Thank goodness.

The key characteristic of a raglan pullover is the sloping seams that run diagonally from the bottom of the armhole and up across the collarbone to the neckline. A raglan pullover has four raglan seams – two at the front and two at the
back. To give them their shape, you decrease if knitting from bottom to top
and increase if knitting from top to bottom – on both sides of the middle of
the seam. In design schools this is called *fashioning*.

The raglan sleeves of The Carpe Diem Sweater (p. 252) are knitted with increases and decreases.

INCREASING AND DECREASING

If your knitting is shaped by decreasing and increasing instead of cutting off, sewing and cutting to size, it is *fully fashioned*. Want a pullover with an A line? Balloon sleeves? A great big, useless vest (like the first garment I ever knitted)? Then decreasing and increasing are the answer.

Two ways to decrease

To decrease (dec) means to reduce the number of stitches.
There are various way of doing this. The easiest is to knit two stitches together.

The abbreviation for this is: k2 tog or p2 tog

You can make your decrease slope neatly to the left or the right, so it looks tidy. This is how you do it:

Decrease with a slope to the right: k2 tog

Decrease with a slope to the left: sl1 k1 psso (slip one stitch, knit one, pass the slipped stitch over).

One way to increase

To increase (inc) means to increase the number of stitches. I use one method for this, but if you've learned another method, use it. It won't affect the design.

inc 1: Pick up the thread between two stitches (from the front using your left needle) and knit into the back of the loop to form a stitch.

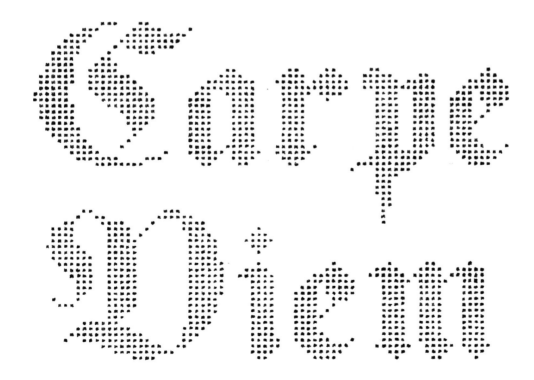

The extra cast-on stitches on the front of the
No Limits Sweater (p. 166) give it a nice round form.

CASTING ON EXTRA STITCHES

We use this technique to add several stitches at once. For example,
on the No Limits Sweater (p. 166).

This is how to do it:

1   Hold the needle needing the extra stitches in your right hand and wind the yarn
     around your thumb.

2   Insert the needle from below through the loop on your thumb. Slide your thumb
     out of the loop and pull the new stitch tight so on the needle. Repeat until you've
     added the right number of stitches.

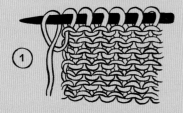
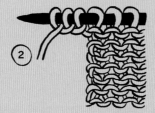

CORRECTING MISTAKES

Okay, this chapter is necessary – even though I always insist you should accept your mistakes and learn to love them. But there are exceptions, of course, and sometimes you really do have to pick up a dropped stitch or unravel a few rows to redo one particular row and "save" the garment.

How to pick up a dropped stitch in stocking stitch, in four steps

1   Work with the right side of your knitting facing you and the horizontal thread behind the dropped stitch. Pick up the horizontal thread with your left needle.

2   From the front, insert the right needle into the dropped stitch and under the horizontal thread.

3   Take the left needle out from under the thread and insert it over the thread into the back of the dropped stitch. Then use it to lift the dropped stitch up and over the horizontal thread that's across the right needle. When you've lifted the stitch over the end of the right needle, you'll have secured your dropped stitch.

4   Next, you need to transfer the secured stitch to your left needle. To do this, insert the left needle into the front of it and slide it off the right needle. You're now ready to carry on knitting.

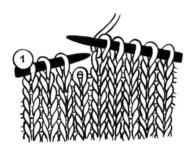

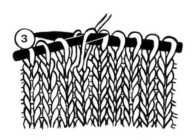

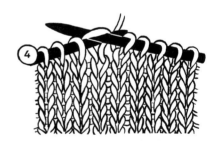

Dropped purl stitches should be picked up from the right side of the work if possible. Turn your knitting carefully so the stitch doesn't slip even further, then secure the stitch as outlined in steps 1-4 above. Turn your work back before continuing to knit.

If you're unlucky, the dropped stitch can descend over more than one row. In this case, it's easier to retrieve it with a crochet hook (p. 64). I always found it rather funny, although it's not all that funny when you drop a stitch, of course.

Picking up a dropped stitch over several rows, in four steps

1 On the right side of your work, a dropped stitch over several rows looks like a ladder. First, make sure the bottom horizontal thread of the ladder is behind the dropped stitch.

2 Pick up the dropped stitch along with the nearest horizontal thread using a crochet hook. Then pull the horizontal thread forwards through the stitch. Now you have secured the first stitch of the ladder.

3 Carry on in the same way, lifting one stitch after another with the crochet hook until you get to the top of the ladder and there are no more dropped stitches left.

4 Insert the left needle into the stitch from the front and slide the stitch onto the left needle. Now you can carry on knitting.

If you have to pick up purl stitches that have dropped down several rows, you'll find it much easier to work with the right side of your knitting facing you. Turn the knitting carefully, follow the steps listed above and then turn it back to carry on knitting.

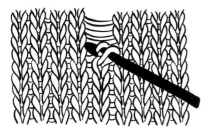

Chosen the wrong colour yarn? Got the wrong tension? Made the garment too wide? You can unravel whole rows or rounds of your knitting:

Unravelling several rows/rounds in two steps

1 Pull the needles out of your knitting. Choose a row/round a few centimetres lower down, where the stitches are well defined – where you can easily see how each one lies so you don't end up in the wrong row or round when you pick up the stitches again. This is best done with the right side of your knitting facing you. That's always the easiest.

2 In the row you've chosen, insert the needle through the right-hand loop of the V that forms each stitch in that row/round – and ONLY the right loop. Make sure you don't miss any stitches or you'll end up with dropped stitches. And don't split the yarn with the tip of your needle. When you've inserted the needle through every stitch in that row/round, you can unravel the knitting as far as the needle. The stitches are now neatly lined up on the needle, ready for you to get started again.

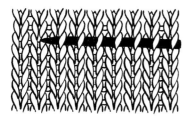

Yes, I drop stitches too! This is The Bad Idea Top (p. 226), knitted in the Bad Idea Scrap technique (p. 110).

Darning in the ends

Darn in the yarn ends on the wrong side of your work, following the arc of the stitches. I always say four stitches away and four back again, inserting the needle through the same stitch.

 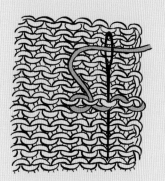

KNITTING THE RIGHT SIZE

I've spent endless hours of my life not liking the way I look. In fact, I used to be so hard on myself that I developed an eating disorder and needed out-patient treatment. So I spent an entire year concentrating only on gaining weight, self-reflection, my body and nutrition. When I couldn't function like the people I kept comparing myself to, I felt a terrible sense of defeat. Today I realise it was a great achievement to overcome this illness and pick myself up again. Stronger, wiser and healthier. That year helped make me the person I am today: a mother, an individual, a knitter.

I'm very aware of how I look and have gradually learned to make the most of my good points. It's taken a mere 36 years to get this far. I have small, almost non-existent breasts. So, I often wear closely-fitting tops so there's at least a hint that they are there. I spent my entire life longing for a real cleavage, just for one single day! Please! But as we know, the grass is always greener on the other side. I also have very short legs. Now you're probably thinking "Shut up! No, you haven't!" But I have, honestly. I'm just extremely good at making them look longer than they are – by wearing high-waist bottoms and crop tops. What are your best features? Mine are my sense of humour and my waist. So I emphasise both.

A good friend once said to me – she was truly tired of the layered look – that she couldn't understand why I insisted on hiding myself. She said I should show myself instead and be proud as I might never look better than I did at that moment and it would be a pity not to waste that. If I ask my other half whether he likes the clothes I've bought, made or am wearing, he often says: "Sure. They're pretty. But you're prettier." Aaaaaaah!

Do you wear XS or XXXXL? Or M – which is in the middle of the sizes table but is not really the middle at all? If you ask me, the time for size listings is over – because they can be discriminating and misleading. They imply you belong to a particular size group based on certain standard measurements that may not fit you at all, or that probably aren't the standard anyway. We look the way we look, and one size is no better than another. If you're not happy with your body, wish you had bigger breasts or a weighed few kilos less, it would be easier if your clothes didn't constantly remind you of the fact. A different sizing system might get rid of at least of this negative awareness.

That's why I decided to list sizes in numbers instead. So in this book XS, S, M, L, XL, XXL, XXXL, XXXXL are 1, 2, 3, 4, 5, 6, 7, 8 – because I believe it makes sense. That means you'll just have to take your own measurements, haha.

Everyone loves crisps! And just remember to love yourself as much as you love *Sour Cream and Onion.*

EASE OF MOVEMENT

To find the right size for your own knitted garment, you'll need to bear a few things in mind. One of the most important is *positive ease*, a comfortable size you can move in, in other words. Positive ease is a fairly new term to me, although I've always worked with it in mind – I just never knew it had such a fancy name.

Anyway, *positive ease* is the difference between your body measurements and the measurements of the pullover. The extra centimetres allow you to move easily in a knitted garment – assuming it isn't too tight. As a rule of thumb, that should be between 5 and 10 cm. So, for your pullover, choose the size of your bust measurement plus 5 to 10 cm for *positive ease*.

Example: If your chest is 98 cm, choose a size with a chest measurement of between 103 and 108 cm. If you want the garment to be wider still, choose a size with even more ease of movement.

Negative ease means a garment is smaller than your body. The term is often used for close-fitting items from stretch material or similar.

Too much beer and chicken nuggets have a strange effect on your glow. My beauty routine consists of a trip to the toilet and a cup of Nescafé, if you're interested.

TAKING MEASUREMENTS

Take your own measurements first, preferably standing in front of a mirror, in your underwear or something close-fitting. Take your chest measurement, overall length and arm length. Here's how:

Chest measurement: Put the tape measure around the widest part of your chest – but don't pull it too tight. Compare your measurement with what's in the pattern instructions. If you want the pullover to be close-fitting, the chest measurement of the garment should be 5–7 cm larger than your chest. If you prefer a normal *loose fit*, it should be about 10 cm bigger. For *oversize* go for 15–20 cm larger. If you have a small chest, consider shortening the front and back up to the armholes by a few centimetres. If you have a large chest, you may need to knit a few centimetres more to accommodate it.

Overall length: Measure from the middle of your shoulders down to where the pullover should finish – to the bottom edge, in other words. Want the pullover to cover your backside and keep it warm? Or should it only go as far as your hips? Measure the length you want and compare it with the "overall length" in the pattern. If you want your garment longer or shorter, knit a few centimetres more or less than the pattern says up to the armholes. That will give you a back and front in the right length. So, if the pattern says knit 35 cm up to the armhole but you want your pullover 5 cm longer, you'll need to knit 40 cm instead. For a shorter pullover, knit shorter.

Arm length: Measure your arm from wrist to armpit. Compare your measurement with what the pattern says and lengthen or shorten the sleeve as described above. You can also try out the sleeve length while you're knitting.

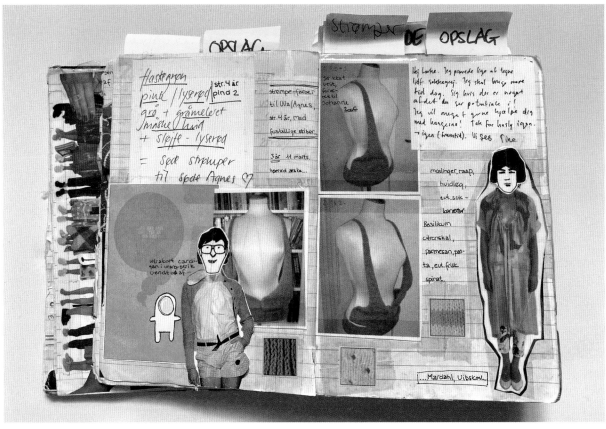

Chapter 3
Colours and Sketches

"Colours are a medium – like a great big party. It really doesn't matter if you can draw or not, because remember: you're good enough just the way you are."

COLOURS

The Carpe Diem Sweater (p. 252) made using the Bad Idea Scrap technique (p. 110).

There are quite a few things I'm really not very good at: dexterity, working under pressure and going home early from town, for example. But colours are something I am good at. And I'm not afraid to say it. If you can do something well, you owe it to yourself to say it out loud.

Your sense of colour is mainly a matter of sensuousness, self-confidence and the ability to visualise things. Follow your instinct. That's important. Otherwise the result will be rubbish. Whenever I took other people's advice about colours, the design always ended up hideous. Without exception. Because it wasn't my vision, my idea or my taste. In short, it just wasn't me. So on this occasion, take my advice!

If you like to experiment and work methodically to develop your own designs and ideas, this chapter is for you. If not, carry on reading anyway because there are some really great tips hidden away amongst my scribblings.

Colour genius or not, there are a few tricks that will really make sure the combinations you choose really hit the spot. Here are my tips and techniques:

- **Don't be afraid:** Throw yourself into it. Combine orange with brown, lime green with fuchsia, beige with another beige. Fear just holds you back. So be bold. I intentionally choose colours that don't go together – because I don't want to go with the flow. But it's easier said than done, as we tend to choose things that are pretty. Instead, just close your eyes and choose your yarns by taking a "lucky dip" approach. We don't do "nice" here!

- **Look at the colours in their context:** The colours you've chosen should relate to each other somehow. Do they shout at each other like yellow and blue? Or whisper like delicate pink and beige? Think about how they look and how that fits in with your vision. Question your choices and find your own answers.

- **Coordinate the colours:** Mixing colours is like mixing ingredients. Think of them as a composition of sweet, salty, fatty and sour. What flavour are you looking for?

- **Work with contrasts:** Contrasts will give the finished result dynamism and character. They don't have to be stark, like yellow and blue – you could just choose a cooler and a warmer shade of white.

Pretty samples of
rolled-up yarns.
Save them!

<

Spread out your
yarns in front of you.
It'll help you see
things more clearly.

>

- **Try out your ideas:** Even when you think your first colour composition is ready, double-check if should be a little warmer or brighter, maybe?

- **Visualise:** Imagine the finished item in different colour combinations. Wind balls of samples or draw colour gradients to help you visualise it. Then choose the colours you find most exciting or that really give you a buzz, even if you're not quite sure at this stage.

- **Analysis is your friend:** What are you aiming for, and what can help you achieve it? A pullover in autumn colours? Then what colours do you associate with autumn? How many do you plan to use, and why? How firm or soft do you want your pullover to be? How many dark or light colours do you want to use? Do you want to combine them?

- **Winding samples:** It's the oldest trick in the book – because it works! Oh boy, have I spent many happy hours with the ersatz activity of just winding yarn samples. Instead of doing what I did as a poor design student – which was to use free postcards with colours and lettering on them – it's better to invest in some thick white card for this. Cut it into smallish rectangles and wind the yarns and colours you're planning around them. Fix the threads on the back with sticky tape. Wound samples help you visualise your ideas. Try out stripes and larger or smaller sections in different colours. It's a brilliant way of testing your ideas. And make sure you save your samples – you never know when they might come in handy. And they look great too.

- **Lay out your yarns:** The easiest way is often the most effective, and this is the trick I use most often. Arrange lots of different-coloured yarns on the table or floor. Mix and match them. Take some out. Play around to your heart's content and follow your intuition. Quite often, I'm really surprised at what comes out when I use this method. I'll suddenly find a brown next to a pink and a green. *Seriously?* And that's why it works! You make different, better decisions because you had more options to choose from.

- **Choose flexibly:** One cool method of choosing colours is something I learned at design school. Flexible searching is a good way of homing in on colour inspirations so you can really see what they look like. For this technique, you need more white card, ideally A4 or A3 size. Now, with a cutter or scalpel, cut a square about 5 x 5 or 8 x 8 cm – or whatever size you like – out of the middle. The larger the square, the more you'll be able to see. Now lay your square on top of your favourite picture, colour photo, slice of pizza or whatever. Try out your flexible viewfinder in all sorts of places. Photograph what you see with your phone so you don't forget and can compare the different squares afterwards. The big white frame keeps out colour noise and helps you recognise new colour combinations in familiar things.

Here are my books
from 2012. They
are still intact!

SKETCH BOOKS – OR PROCESS BOOKS

Even just the mention of the word "sketch book" gives me stomach ache. Sketch books are what artists, great designers, architects and other creative geniuses work with. People who can knock out fantastic drawings of their ideas whenever they like. So they automatically put you under pressure. But that's not actually how it works. Believe me. It takes years to get to know yourself and find your own way of sketching. As I now know. I spent most of my youth and adult life struggling with my own inferiority complex around drawing and other forms of visualisation – mostly because I wanted to be as good as everyone else. But who is everyone else, exactly? They're just other people whom I thought had got it right. We all know how that feels, right?

I studied at the *The Royal Danish Academy of Fine Arts, School of Design* and have a *Master of Arts in Design*. But that only cranks the creative pressure up even more. I might just as well have been to the *Hogwarts School of Witchcraft and Wizardry*. Just kidding. That doesn't sound very earnest or dignified – but humour always helps against pressure. I mostly just tell people I went to design school. That's more suitable. A school where you study design.

81

I can't remember where I got the word "process book" from, but I like it much better than "sketch book". "Process book" suggests a journey, that you're on your way but not quite there yet. As people, women, mothers and friends, we constantly have to perform, professionally and privately, and to produce things, show results, be perfect and successful. Well, you can forget that! Instead, let's just concentrate on the process and journey that will take us to where we want to be. That way, our projects are more likely to succeed and we'll enjoy them. I've been on my way for years already and still haven't quite got there.

A process book is a sort of creative diary with observations, ideas and other stuff. Stuff you find important at that moment and can't let go of. One of my former teachers compared the process book with money in the bank, and I agree. A process book is like putting money aside for your dentist's bill or saving for 100,000 years to get a Prada handbag. Sorting your finances. But this is about sorting your brainwaves and ideas because when you've written them down, you'll have room for more, possibly better and even more ingenious ones. The point is: put them aside and save them.

The same teacher told me to keep calm, relax a bit and analyse my work better. Instead of knitting 100 mediocre tension squares I should concentrate and knit five good ones – otherwise I'd need ten rubbish bins for all my experiments and end up burned-out by the time I was thirty. That's what my teacher said! I'm still trying to follow his advice but am just not much good at it. I'll try again next Monday.

I've been filling process books for as long as I can remember. It's in my blood. And I still use almost all of them. Some are naive, highly personal and detailed, others contain sober instructions. I have design process books and ones that just ought to be binned, whose sole purpose is to bring order to my muddled brain. I've experimented with different formats too, had a crisis, tried a new format, then had another crisis…

When I leaf through all my process books, from first to last, it's easy to recognise the common thread. Really. Incredibly easy. My books have developed with me. I've grown up from a child to a young person to an adult, and it's all there in the books. It's fantastic!

Best, *Dalai* Lærke

During all those years at design school, I sat next to Josefine and Miranda, two incredibly talented print designers. They were my closest colleagues working in a lonely sector. I still share a workshop with Josefine now, but Miranda moved back to Norway, unfortunately. Not in the least bit amusing, I thought. The way Josefine and Miranda used their process books was amazing. I just sat beside them and got totally pissed off as I scribbled around with my stuff and chucked out one useless pencil drawing after the other. Our teachers were over the moon with their books, but with me, all they did was encourage me to keep trying. I felt like the stupid friend who never gets invited anywhere but whose friendship everybody needs. I kept on trying to copy their methods but went wrong every time. It wasn't until our final exams – after six unbelievably long years – that I realised their books were part of their product as designers, products in their own right, not a means to an end. Ahaaaa! I'd wasted so much valuable energy being miserable and frustrated because I was comparing myself to them. So, what's the moral of the story? Look forwards, not sideways! Do your own thing. Don't compare yourself with others and don't try to be something you're not. There's a reason why you're the way you are and why you can't be good at everything. It's just not possible. And that's how to use a process book.

Best,
Lærke-*Mama*

- **Lower your expectations:** A book doesn't have to look or be a certain way. It's just a tool for you to use, not a product for others to judge. And remember: lots of people you try to imitate are professional designers and had a creative training.

- **Buy yourself a nice notebook:** It'll make you feel good. At least it'll look good on the outside!

- **Save everything:** Whether it's a postcard that cheers you up, a sweet wrapper in pretty colours or a leaf with intricate veins, a small, insignificant everyday thing can be exactly what gives you the idea for your next pullover. The idea for my final collection came from a seashell I'd seen on holiday in Thailand and came to me on the flight home. The trouble is, it was about two weeks too late for my assignment deadline.

- **Write:** Maybe you associate a few words with the postcard, sweet wrapper or leaf. Thoughts, considerations, inspiration as to why you're saving it. Write them down because they'll give you a lovely warm feeling later, when you've forgotten why on earth you stuck that withered leaf in your lovely book.

- **Functionality:** Whether the content of your book is attractive or not doesn't matter. All that counts is whether it does what you want it to.

- **A trick for remembering things:** Use a little box, plastic bag or drawer as interim storage for objects and photos until you stick them in your book. You probably won't always have time to cut things out and stick them in straightaway, but at least they won't get lost.

- **Corrections:** Make a note of any corrections and changes to your various designs and instructions. Your notes will be worth their weight in gold later on, when you've forgotten everything.

- **Keep:** Never bin an experiment. You never know when it might come in handy. Also, always carry a notebook with you – because inspiration can come to you anywhere. It's nigh-on impossible to cart your process book around with you – not even professionals do that. But you can always scribble a note in your book or type it into your phone. Then just stuff the sweet paper or whatever in your pocket and glue into your book later on.

- **Pleasure:** Your process books and notebooks should give you pleasure, not stress you out, overwhelm you or make you miserable. If they do, then forget about them!

DRAWING, COLLAGE AND IN-BETWEEN STUFF

So, what's a process book actually for? To help you improve, of course. And what's the use of improving? Nothing whatsoever! Because the most important thing is to be happy and have fun. I spent years trying to improve – at all the wrong things, mind you – and that's what it taught me. I would waste my time on things that were never going to work anyway, but I still managed to find my way. And I now know pretty much everything – not!

The idea that you have to be able to draw to be a designer or creative is a great big lie. I can't draw, but I've learned a few techniques, and now I just fake it. I kept on putting off my application to design school because I couldn't draw – or rather, I thought I couldn't. But let me tell you a secret: it's not about being able to draw! It's about being able to visualise and communicate your ideas in some way or other, be it by drawing, collage, words, singing or acting. If you're good at drawing, be pleased! And if not, so what?

For the entrance test for design school, we had an interview with two of the professors there. They were supposed to assess our abilities and talent, so we had to bring along a product and two sketch books (process books). I was so nervous I cried the entire way there. One of them spent ages leafing through my books and then said: "Well, I can see you don't do much drawing." Whereupon Lærke, aged 23, answered: "Oh, well, I'm just not very good at it. That's all." The professor opened a drawer, got out an empty sketch book, gave it to me and said: "Then you'd better go home and practise a bit." No more was said. I was done for! I called my mother and cried, telling her they'd never accept me. Incidentally, it took five nerve-racking months for my exam result to come through. Fortunately, they accepted me – but my trauma about drawing had grown to twice the size.

During my first year I had a fantastic teacher who helped me work through my trauma. He was my first really creative teacher, and his worldview was different from anything I'd ever known before. He was the first person to actually represent a system – in this case the educational system –while at the same time prompting me not to give a damn about the system and to take responsibility for myself. In short: to find my own way.

During my first year at design school, we learned basic techniques and methods like croquis, colour theory and various different drawing techniques, including perspective drawing. Ugh! If that kind of thing's your bag, then sorry, but it certainly isn't mine. I'd rather give birth than do a perspective drawing. At least during a birth something happens. Whatever. The task was to sit in a local library and draw the room from three different angles with the correct dimensions and perspectives. Ugh again! We then had to hand in our three drawings to be assessed. It was the worst week of my life, really tough, but I handed in my drawings nonetheless. Then at some point we got our assessments. The teacher said loud and clear: "Just tell me honestly, what were you thinking? You call this good?" I told him I hated drawing and would much rather create a collage. Whereupon he replied that it was up to me, dammit, to find the task interesting and that he didn't care if I could draw or not, as long as I could visualise things in perspective. I could have built a library out of gingerbread and submitted that, as long as the perspective was right, he said. And that was when Lærke suddenly grew up. I could no longer blame things on other people. It was all a

question of practice. And when you've read my tips, you won't be able to blame other people any more either.

So I practised my limited drawing skills so I could at least be good at drawing pullovers. But that's the limit of my ability. But I'm very good at sketching and visualising material – I knit neat samples and make collages with them, in other words.

- **Try out different drawing implements:** Perhaps you can work better with some than others. I can't get on with drawing in pencil but like using felt-tip pens and chunky ballpoints.

- **Invest in a good felt-tip pen, eraser and ballpoint:** Or in whatever you like using best. I like thick felt-tip pens for outlines and rough features, and thin fineliners for the details.

- **Use different sizes of tip:** Using different thicknesses of felt-tip pen, ballpoint or pencil in a single drawing will lend your work depth and perspective and look super-professional.

- **Practise:** Think about what you'd like to be able to draw and practise that – and only that. Don't spend your time drawing hands if you really want to be able to draw cool pullovers.

- **Trace things:** If you want to draw a dress, look for a photo of a dress and trace it. Then incorporate your own changes, e.g. lengthen the sleeves, make the dress fuller, etc.

- **Choose templates:** For example, cut figures out of magazines or print some out from the internet that suit the way you express yourself. It will boost your creativity. Or you can trace them.

WORKING WITH COLLAGE

- **Save everything:** Cuttings, photos, little patches, anything you like. Collage is just a cool word for cutting out and sticking.

- **New ways:** Use photos or cuttings of different knitted items and put them together in different ways. Combine things that don't really go together. A pizza as a dress or flowers as sunglasses, for instance. The quirkiest combinations can create associations to make a usable, three-dimensional form.

- **Detail:** Make yourself a flexible viewfinder (p. 80). Put it on your collage and move it around to focus on different details.

- **Work in layers:** Create a collage starting from a figure or spatial form.

- **Document:** Take photos as you go. Your first sketch might turn out to be the best after all.

Chapter 4
The Essence of Lærke Bagger Close Knit

"Just tie knots. The darkest scrap yarn secrets."

YARN TYPES

Yarn is the very best thing in all the world. It's the beginning and source of everything. I love all yarns, just like I love all people. Cotton, wool, mohair, special-effect yarns, acrylic, polyester, you name it. Each has its own justification and its place in the world. Even a neon-coloured print-fur-acrylic yarn deserves to be loved. The only yarn I don't find so great is cashmere, but that's because I could never afford it. So I'm probably just envious. I'm told it's fantastic to knit with.

I know, yawn! But if you do want to replace one type of yarn with another, you need to know what you're doing. I've always just replaced yarns without checking, measuring or counting and have got it wrong plenty of times. So I recommend learning a bit more. Then again, maybe not.

All the yarns used in this book are by Hjertegarn. That makes it incredibly easy to switch between them if you can't get what you need or have found a different amazing yarn in a really cool colour. If you already have some fantastic balls of yarn that you've bought second hand or on the internet, choose one that has roughly the same yardage per 50 or 100 grams as specified in the pattern and is recommended for the same needle size. You'll find the information on the label of the yarn. The vast majority of yarns are available from various manufacturers in more or less similar form.

If you're not interested in knowing about yarn types, ask your local yarn store for help. They're the experts. I used to work at *Nicoline Garn*, a yarn store in Nørrebro in Copenhagen. We spent 75 percent of our time helping customers find alternative yarns. It was a really great job, but unfortunately I had to stop when I got pregnant because after a while, I could only sell yarn sitting down.

Although I worked in a wool shop, I'm not an expert when it comes to materials. For example, I've no idea how silk yarns are manufactured. In materials classes at design school, I mostly sat at the back and spent my time texting my friend, who was a student at the School of Architecture. We texted about the cute guys we'd met and where to go for a drink. At the time, of course, I thought cute guys and drinks were more important than materials. In fact, I still think that even today despite being ten years older – which means I ought to be ten years smarter.

I never was interested in the scientific or technical side of yarns. For me, materials and yarns were always something sensuous and intuitive. A passion. A need. When I'm choosing a yarn, I think to myself: "I want a yarn in this colour. Okay, so it's polyacrylic, but who cares?" I've always mixed, used and treated different yarn types however I like, and only looked at the label afterwards. Just like I mix my drinks when I go out. It's led to countless "Oh shiiit!" moments but to just as many crazy gifts as well. At Design School 'gifts' was what we used to call mistakes and *f*** ups* that ended well.

Selection of different types and colours of yarn for The Bad Idea Top (p. 226). The main colours are pink, yellow and beige.

Wool

Wool is an animal fibre that mostly comes from sheep or goats. It's elastic and good for beginners because it can be pulled into shape nicely. So when you've finished, your work will look more regular than with cotton. When you knit with wool, the result is usually really lovely.

MY FAVOURITE WOOLS

- **Merino wool:** Super-soft and really hard to go wrong with.

- **South American sheep's wool:** This is just *nice* and looks *old school*, really granny-like.

- **Wick wool:** Use needle size 6–7. Knits up really fast. It's unspun, thick and soft.

laerkebagger ...

Vis indblik   Promover

 Synes godt om fra **iksiks** og **165 andre**

laerkebagger Never get high on your own supply
#fringes# knitwear #fur #laerkebagger

Vis alle 3 kommentarer

29. juni 2015

The Viking fur.
Thank you, Sune,
for recognising
a bit of Danish
history here.

I'm a fan of wool. You can hardly fault wool, and you don't have to be a millionaire to work with it. Unless it's cashmere or alpaca, that is. Cashmere was never a favourite of mine because it's so damned expensive. The price is too much of an issue for me, so I can never relax if I'm designing for cashmere or alpaca. Also, alpaca has too many fine hairs so it makes far too many dust bunnies. Other fibres I don't care about and know absolutely nothing about are silk and linen. Which also has something to do with envy.

Mohair

Mohair is also wool – in a way. It comes from the angora goat but is often mixed with silk or polyacrylic to make it more resilient. I am pretty crazy about mohair, and once I'd finally accepted I'd have fluff in my mouth all the time, my euphoria knew no bounds. My father Henning and my partner Sune, however, are the biggest mohair-haters in the world because of all the fluff, *cough*. My father wouldn't let me knit mohair in his car and insists on calling it "infernal stuff". Even in my own home I'm banned from the sofa when knitting mohair. My husband is against my knitting anything at all on the sofa, in fact, unless it's cotton, which doesn't make any fluff at all. So I always sit on the floor when I'm knitting. But when I'm alone at home, of course, I always sit on the sofa. Mohair is fantastic to knit and makes a great auxiliary yarn because it's so fine and delicate, and it gives the design a very personal touch.

Cotton

Cotton is for more experienced knitters. It's not elastic, so it takes far more technical skill to knit evenly. In other words, you have to have your grip and movements well under control. But cotton does fall very attractively and naturally whereas wool tends to look a bit heavier.

Cotton isn't suitable for large or heavy pullovers, covers or cushions – as I learned from bitter experience. For my final exam I knitted a floor-length fur coat in cotton with extra threads knitted into it. The coat turned out so heavy that the model wearing it could hardly stand up. Poor girl. She had to leap around with about five kilos on her back. What's more, the coat was pretty ugly. When I came home from design school one evening and proudly showed it to my boyfriend, he said he loved the way I'd recreated a piece of Danish history: he said it looked like something from the Viking age.

Special-effect yarns

Acrylic, fur, print and nylon. I love anything quirky, and when I see all the cool, freaky, sexy special-effect yarns that are around, I get really excited. Without them, there would be no Lærke Bagger. Special-effect yarns are not considered as fine as wool, mohair and cotton – which is really sad because there's truly nothing cooler than a fur yarn in neon colours that screams, "Look what I've made, and I'm proud of it."

Look at your yarns, rummage around in your collection and re-arrange them. That way you'll keep coming up with new ideas for colour combinations.

Different yarns are good for different things and come at different prices. And let's face it, we all have our favourites. You don't have to be a millionaire to knit something awesome. My designs are made in a way that means you can use pretty well any yarn for any pattern. If you hate wool but love acrylic, then just use that (p. 263). Some designs look better in one yarn than another – and I give that information in my patterns. For example, don't knit with beads and 100 % cotton. It will turn out ugly and incredibly heavy and go all baggy after a while.

Throughout my knitting career, I've often been told never to mix different yarn types and colours: "You can't knit wool and cotton together!" or "You can't mix acrylic with wool and cotton!" But quite honestly, why not? And besides, who are you to tell me what to do? I've always combined yarns the way I like. And so should you, if you ask me. Just do what you like. You know best! And besides, who am I to tell you what to do?

THE BASE COLOUR

Almost everything I knit has a single colour as the basis. You might not believe it, but there is method in my madness. The base colour is your basic yarn, a sort of common thread running through the entire knitted item. It adds a touch of calm, a break and creates a space to let all the crazy colours, textures and forms really stand out. You need a calming element as a contrast to all the madness, otherwise your garment will turn out ugly. I love expressiveness, but the expressiveness has to be tamed.

The basic yarn in my designs is like the salt, pepper and sugar in a delicious gravy. The most important thing is good ingredients and a long cooking time, but your gravy won't be any good without seasoning. Sometimes it will need a lot of salt, pepper or sugar, other times just a little.

And sometimes the only thing that will rescue your gravy is a good dollop of Heinz tomato ketchup. In my designs, the basic yarn regulates the expression of a piece in the same way. Crank things up, tone them down, correct and perfect them, adapt and harmonise.

Best,
Lærke *the Poet*

I moved to Copenhagen in my early twenties. At that time, I normally used to knit with acrylic yarns, which I bought second hand, or with yarn I'd borrowed from my mother while visiting home. I couldn't bring myself to throw away the leftovers. They cost money and I didn't want to waste anything, so I saved them without knowing what for. One day I knotted them together and found there was enough for an entire ball of yarn. I knitted it up and have saved everything longer than 8 cm ever since. I had started knitting with yarn scraps.

SCRAP YARN

The cool name for yarn made up of odds and ends is *scrap yarn*. It includes:
- Cut-off ends of threads
- Annoying leftover balls of yarn
- Yarns from finished, gone-wrong knitting projects
- Bad buys because a friend persuaded you coral pink really is your colour
- Alpaca yarn, before you realised all the loose hairs make an incredible amount of dust
- Impulse purchases – single balls of yarn in cute colours, in other words. "I could knit a hat with that!" Haha!
- The enormous bag of yarn you got from your mother's friend – thanks so much, by the way, because without it, I couldn't knit my way through the next century
- Gone-wrong projects that you've unravelled
- Balls of yarn with different lot numbers
- Yarn from second-hand shops – a great life hack!

In short: Scrap yarn is any yarn that's doomed to be disposed of.

A TIP FOR ACQUIRING SCRAP YARN

- If you think you haven't got enough scrap yarn or want other colours and types, then swap little skeins or cut-off thread ends with friends or the knitting club. It's a great way to grow your collection. Alternatively, suck up to someone who has a bigger collection than you. I've done well that way. And yes, buy second hand. But whatever you do, remember to put it in the freezer at minus 18 degrees or more for a week to kill off any moths or other creatures that may be lurking in it.

A whole lot of cut threads waiting to be knotted together to All Over skeins (p. 106).

AN INTRODUCTION TO SCRAP TECHNIQUES

I use scrap yarn in a thousand different and complex ways but only have three basic techniques:

- **ATS**
- **All Over**
- **Bad Idea**

The most fascinating thing about *scrap yarn* is that your knitting will be incredibly individual. A pullover I knit will look quite different from one my mother has knitted, and hers will look different from what you knit. Designing something means putting some of yourself, your style, your temperament, your favourite colours, your mood and your yarn stocks into it. Together, these things will then determine the expression of your pullover. When you knit with *scrap yarn*, every design will be different and highly individual.

A *scrap yarn* pullover will also be a personal record of your previous knitting projects, successful or not. You'll see a yarn in it and think: "Oh yes – that pink wool was SO pretty." Also, when I look at my Scrap projects, I can tell which ones I knitted in a good mood and which ones I knitted when life was getting me down.

For the patterns in this book, you can use whatever Scrap techniques you like and then adapt the design accordingly. Almost all the patterns and Scrap techniques in this book go together, and any exceptions are noted in the instructions. So, go for it! Knit different yarn types and thicknesses in a single design. The patterns are perfect for it!

When I was young, I had an eating disorder and lived by specific and fanatically devised rules. I never deviated from them. It's a long story, of course, but one with a happy ending. Nonetheless, my eating disorder will always be a part of who I am and how I work. So today, my only rule is: there are no rules. Rules make my hair stand on end. Nowadays I eat according to the principle of "everything in moderation". And that's how I knit as well. If I fancy chicken nuggets for breakfast or nachos and dip for lunch, then that's what I eat. But then I have to eat lots of vegetables for supper. If I want to knit a glittery thread for size 2 needles with size 6 needles, I have to make sure I compensate by adding in a thick strand of brown wool.

Whether you follow all, some or none of the principles of my three Scrap techniques is entirely up to you. Personally, I'm very flexible, because I decide by instinct and gut feeling.

Whatever you do, be open, make a start and don't overthink things. Otherwise they'll get difficult. Switch your brain off and gut feeling on: What makes you happy? What feels right? And don't be afraid of making mistakes. You'll learn from them and improve. Instead, make your mistakes a part of your design. It would be much worse if you never made any. It would be boring, in fact.

JUST TIE KNOTS

The common element in the three Scrap techniques is the knots – loved and loathed from coast to coast. If you follow my instructions, there will be no need to worry about them coming undone. I know because I've been tying knots since the days when the Spice Girls were on MTV. I was most definitely Sporty Spice!

I am also a control freak. And I'd hazard a guess that most crafters are. See knitting as a journey of self-development. You can't control where a knot will land, so just accept it. Push it through to the back – even though there's an 80-percent chance it will slip to the front again. See the lack of control as a tribute to the fallible and real. The knots will be visible on both the front and the back of your knitting and will add a dynamic element to it. They'll bring a bit of life to what you've made and show it was hand-crafted with love – or possibly anger, frustration and tears. Mistakes reflect our being and make things interesting. Perfection is boring. Mistakes makes us human. So let go of your thoughts and your self-control and enjoy being your real self through knitting. You don't have to achieve anything. Knitting is your oasis – and if you really hate the knots, then push them through to the back. No sweat.

Best,
Lærke *the life coach*

Tying knots in six steps

1 Place the two ends you want to knot next to each other, parallel.

2 Tie a normal knot – which I call a "parallel knot".

3 Take two ends and cross them over.

4 Tie them in a simple knot – which I call a "cross knot". Pull it tight.

5 Put the ends parallel to each other again and tie another parallel knot.

6 Pull it tight and cut off the ends 2-3 mm away from the knot.

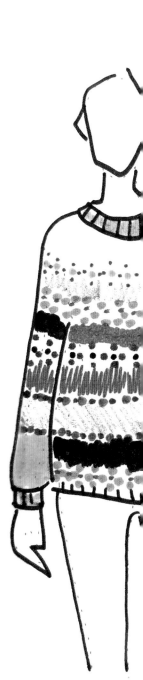

Is the knot making a hole? Or making your stitches go uneven? Or refusing to sit neatly? If so, that's easy to fix with the thread you're knitting with: just tug it a bit or pull it a bit tighter as you knit the stitch so the knot lands where you want it. If you cut off the loose ends before you start knitting, it makes the knot easier to position.

You can also tie knots on cast-on and cast-off edges, around armholes and with all the ends that are left dangling after you've finished your garment. To make sure nothing comes undone, split the end of the thread in two. Sew one end through the back of a few stitches. Then do the same with the other, ending close to the first one. Tie the two ends together and cut them off.

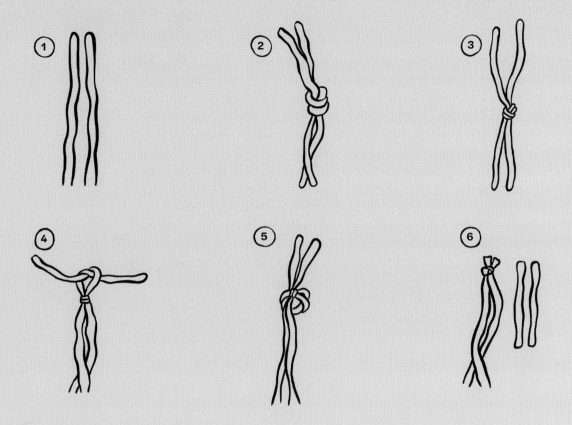

Dos and don'ts of knotting

- Don't knot a very fine yarn with very thick one. The knot won't hold. Instead, use a medium-strength thread to link them.

- Don't knot super-smooth yarns like viscose because the knot won't hold. If you can't live without smooth yarn — and it does sometimes happen — link the threads with an auxiliary thread.

- Always pull the threads of the knot tight. Very important!

- Always join two ends of yarn with at least three knots.

- Tie the knots in whatever way suits you best. I like normal parallel knots and cross knots best. But if you're a sailor or girl scout, you can probably excel with more advanced techniques.

- Keep your trimmed-off thread ends. You can card them to make new yarn or use them as stuffing for a teddy bear. Or as Barbie spaghetti.

ATS SCRAP TECHNIQUE

The Alone Together Sweater was designed to offer hope and diversion in the uncertain times of the first coronavirus lockdown in March 2020. I developed and knitted the design in just five days while on parental leave with my son Lars, who was three months old. I also had my four-year-old daughter Lulu at home. I knitted the Alone Together Sweater with yarn from my mum and dad's house, where we were visiting when we couldn't go out because of the virus. I wrote a pattern for people to knit with whatever they had lying around at home. My plan was to give away my Alone Together Sweater on Instagram. I wanted to create a global online community where people could spend an uncertain and scary time doing something positive. The look of the pullover depended on the knitter's own style, temperament, colour preferences and yarn, so all the pullovers people made turned out completely different and very personal.

SEE #ALONETOGETHERSWEATER ON INSTAGRAM

- Be inspired by others and knit an ATS. It's crazy how enthusiastic everyone is!

The Alone Together Sweater is knitted with my first Scrap technique. All you do is cut off the basic yarn, knot on a bit of another yarn, and then re-attach your basic yarn to that (p. 100).

After a while I got tired of saying "Alone Together Sweater" – although the name really does describe the lockdown situation we were all in at the time. It's just that saying it didn't feel good. It was like speaking with two cherry tomatoes in your mouth. So I started calling it "ATS" for short.

The ATS technique is the easiest of my Scrap techniques because you can decide for yourself how much – or how little – time to invest. You can make it really elaborate or just reduce it to a minimum. The colours are easy to control too because you just quietly tie scrap threads into your basic yarn as you knit.

If you find the whole idea of "me and *scrap yarn*" too challenging, the ATS technique is a good place to start.

The original
#AloneTogether
Sweater. With white
as the base colour
and scrap threads
in all sorts of other
colours added in.

11.38

Vis indblik

Promover

 Synes godt om fra **klara_lilja** og **6.507 andre**

laerkebagger Ok so almoooost there, after speedknitting
for 5 days. Only need to finish the ribbing on the sleeves.
Im gonna be totally honest with you guys, I'm just... mere

Vis alle 330 kommentarer

103

The Bad Idea Top
(p. 226), knitted
using the ATS Scrap
technique (p. 102).

Introduction to ATS

Follow any or all of the principles listed here in whatever way you like. I'm
sure the result will be awesome whatever you do. The most important thing
is to have fun:

- **Colour profile:** Your colour profile consists of all the colours you're going
  to knit together – your base colour and the colours of your scrap yarns,
  in other words. So, decide on one – or none at all. Sometimes I work with
  every colour under the sun. Other times I choose between 10 and 20 colours
  or shades and use some more than others. But pink is almost always one of
  them, *lol!* You can also limit yourself to three, five or seven colours if you
  prefer. *The sky's the limit.*
- **Decide on your base colour:** Your base colour is fundamental to your garment. A muted grey, beige or brown will be calm. But you can also go for
  more of a contrast, with white or black. Or go all out and use something like
  pink or green as your base colour. Follow your heart and you can't go wrong.
- **Scrap threads 8–50 cm long:** Cut your scrap threads into lots of different
  lengths because the unevenness will create the coolest look. Use lots
  of different types and thicknesses of yarn. It'll add life and lightness to
  your design.
- **Knit with the basic yarn and knot the scrap threads in:** As you knit – be it
  with one thread or several – cut the basic yarn off from time to time and tie
  in a scrap thread. Re-attach the basic yarn to the other end of it (p. 102).
- **Use different colours and yarn types:** Use your favourite colours and add in
  a colour you hate from time to time. That will make the end result even more
  wicked. I almost always work with a 60/40 weighting: 60 percent don't-give-a-
  damn colours, such as white, beige, grey, brown, black and khaki, and 40 percent spice-of-life colours, like pink, blue, red, yellow and green.
- **Use different numbers of scrap threads:** Because a yoke has more stitches per
  round than a sleeve, it's best to use less of your base colour between the scrap
  threads on the sleeves so they look more like yoke. Experiment a bit and you'll
  soon work it out.
- **Knit the rib sections separately (p. 35) and crochet them on (p. 49):** If you
  don't, your ATS knitting could end up looking like something you made in
  year five at school.

ATS is like painting with yarn. Add a piece of scrap in every second, fourth
or seventh round or row. Alternatively, just switch off your brain and go wherever your mood takes you. I like it best when I can't work out the pattern. So
I constantly break my rhythm and add in a scrap thread, sometimes on every
row, then on every second row, and then knit an entire row without adding
anything in, etc.

ALL OVER SCRAP TECHNIQUE

All Over Scrap is like a naughty little sister. A bit noisy, taking all your time and attention, and difficult to control. But that's what makes it such fun, and so individual and lovable. The All Over technique can be a thread integrated at various points all over something you're knitting with a single thread, or an auxiliary thread to complement the basic yarn.

Basically, the All Over technique is self-made yarn. You wind your own ball of it by knotting long and short lengths of yarn together. I know what you're going to say now: "Oh no! It will take far too long to wind my own balls of yarn!" Well, all I can say is, your patience will be well rewarded. It's worth the effort, I promise.

The All Over technique is not so much about the finished product but about your process, vision and the ritual preparations before casting on for your new knitting project. It's about your sometimes unrealistic vision of the finished product. Winding your first ball, casting on and discovering your knitting is too thin, too long or too ugly is all part of the process. And so is correcting mistakes, giving yourself an occasional pat on the back, starting over, and experiencing the pleasure of finding the form you want. And to be quite honest, the All Over technique doesn't take any longer. Making things by hand just is a slow process.

The randomness of the colour combination is incredibly liberating and but can also be quite nerve-racking. At some point, you're bound to feel really fed up with a sequence in your knitting – but only briefly because the next one will have you jumping for joy. There's never a dull moment with All Over.

Introduction to All Over

- **Decide on your colour profile:** Do you even want one, or is this going to be a tidying-up or trash project? Either is really cool. Maybe you want to give up control completely and throw in all kinds of colours and yarn types at will? Or perhaps you want something more controlled?

- **Find your way of winding yarn:** Want to work on your project a bit at a time? With smaller skeins, perhaps? Or with really big balls of yarn? Maybe you wind your yarn at school or college? That's what I did, and I ended up having to give up religious education because I'd written too few notes – and because the world and his wife all thought I should knit, of course. Wind your yarn on the bus, in the car or whenever you have a spare five minutes. I always carry a little bag with me whenever I go somewhere where I might have to wait but the wait will probably be too short for knitting yet long enough for me to get tetchy. Wind your skein around four fingers and then tuck the end of the thread in so it doesn't come undone.

- **Use threads 40-100 cm long:** For a varied look, use different lengths of yarn. You can use shorter threads as well, but to be honest, winding a load of 8 cm-long threads into a ball is pretty time-consuming. Save your short threads for an ATS design instead.

Yours truly in the workshop with scrap threads, ready for All Over skeins.

- **Put a heap of threads on the table:** Ideally you need lots of different colours and yarn types, even if you're working with a limited colour profile. Choose two threads and knot them together. Then choose another and knot that one on too – and so on and so forth. I've found that for me, the flow is best if I knot about ten or twelve threads together and trim the ends after that (p. 100). It gives me a better overview of the colour combinations. Personally, I'm completely obsessed with little skeins in different colours because they're so pretty. But the main thing is to find your own personal flow.

- **Change the focus:** When you start winding a new ball, make yourself change the focus. You'll probably find you combine the same colours and yarns every time, so have a good old rummage through your heap of threads as you go and make sure you integrate colours you wouldn't normally choose – in my case beige, grey and brown. Colours like that are essential because otherwise things can get a bit loud.

- **Create a balance:** In each skein of 10-12 threads, include at least one black, one white and a basic colour like grey, beige or brown. That will calm things down and add a little balance so it doesn't get too wild and colourful. But if you're the kind of person who can never get enough colours, just ignore my advice. Don't let me stop you!

- **Coordinating:** If you're knitting faded colours with a subdued base colour, be careful not to include too much black. It'll look too harsh. Instead, add a black thread in every third or fourth skein.

Skeins or balls? That's up to you. Use all colours or just a few shades.

USE YOUR BASIC YARN IN SCRAP SKEINS

- If you're knitting All Over with an auxiliary yarn to accompany the basic yarn, take a few threads of the basic yarn and knot them into the scrap skeins. It will look great and create a balanced overall picture.

BAD IDEA SCRAP TECHNIQUE

The Bad Idea Top in the dress version. You will find the pattern on p. 226.

The Bad Idea technique is a *really good idea!* I developed it during my tender teenage years, when endless plain-knit scarves with colour changes left me with crises of identity. My scarves reflected the fact that I never knew which yarns I could afford or get hold of. So I would start out with a random design, but with built-in principles, and develop a certain logic – basically to avoid producing a scarf that was simply too horrid.

I've kept those scarves and am still fascinated by the uncompromising colour schemes even now: the very *old-school*, summer-cottage look and the plain, almost naive style. And so the past, present and future fused to form a new idea: to knit my own evening dress in just 21 days for the *Elle Style Awards*, where I'd been nominated as Newcomer of the Year, and to blog on Instagram about the impossible process of knitting a garter-stitch dress purely from scrap yarn – with 420 stitches per round, and pleats.

Basically, the Bad Idea technique involves knitting stripes from left-over yarn and making longer or shorter sections based on more or less concrete principles. Psychologically, Bad Idea is very demanding because you need to concentrate all the time on what you're knitting and how you're combining the different colours and yarns. The constant doubt makes it pretty stressful because your knitting will turn out either hideous or absolutely stunning. You're more or less in crisis mode the entire time because every choice you make affects the overall impression of the end result.

The Bad Idea technique is like life: Some times are easy and things run smoothly, others are harder. You have to take things a day, an hour or a stitch at a time. And that's why Bad Idea is my favourite technique. I love the fact that it's difficult and allows me to get in touch with myself – whether in life in general or just while I'm knitting. Whether you're turning, cutting off, changing colour, knotting, stopping, re-working or changing direction, never lose faith in your ability to achieve your goal.

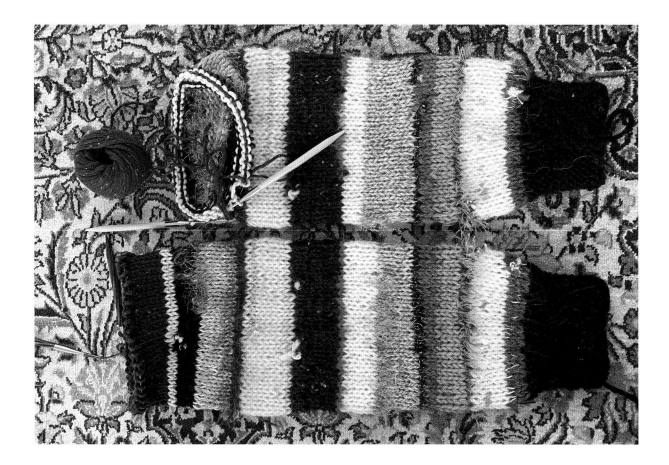

An introduction to Bad Idea

Use a variety of scrap yarns: shortish threads, small skeins, half-balls, whole-balls, *whatever*. And use any thicknesses, types and colours.

- **Find your colour profile:** That means identifying between three and six colours/shades/tones to use as the basic theme colours for your garment. They'll add a bit of calm to your crazy design. I mostly work with whites and blacks as my base colours, depending on what colours I'm keen on at that point or happen to have lying around in my box of odds and ends. I then choose two or three others to go with them. For my Bad Idea Top (p. 226) I chose pink (I always choose pink!), olive green (God knows why) and various shades of brown. Those five colours – white, black, pink, olive and brown – are the dominant ones, the ones to come back to when things get too wild. I use one of the basic yarns as a rest, when I need a pause for thought. And if necessary, I'll buy a ball of basic yarn.

- **Get an overview:** To get an overview of the yarns, colours and types you have, tip them out into a heap or put them in a bag. Mix and match them and look at them as a whole. Do they look too ordinary to bother with or are you overcome by the desire to start knitting? Take some out and add others in. Play around with them and follow your gut feeling. Take some photos with your phone to keep a record of the different colour combinations.

Sleeves for The Bad
Idea Top (p. 226).

- **Inspiration for your colour choice:** You can find inspiration anywhere. In painting, a photo – whatever. And you can change your mind and choose something else whenever you like. That's what I do: "Hey, we need a bit of orange here." Don't be afraid of contrast colours. They'll be awesome! Change colours in the middle of a row, or at the beginning or end. Just cut the thread and knot in a new one (p. 100). Change colours at different places in your knitting to make it more dynamic.

- **Decide on an approximate knitting tension:** And try to follow it more or less. If you can't keep to the tension and the knitting is becoming too tight or too loose, cut the thread. Or unravel a bit if you're way off the mark and then pick up where you left off with a new thread. If you're using a thin-ish yarn, one way of adjusting your tension is by adding in a fine yarn, like silk mohair, mohair or alpaca to make it a bit thicker. If necessary, buy a few balls of thin yarn as a backup. You'll find a use for it.

- **Use special-effect yarns:** Yarns that don't exactly fit in but have plenty of volume and texture form a great contrast to more traditional yarns and are a good way of breaking away from the neat, hand-crafted look. You could include fur, popcorn, print or fringe yarns, for example. You won't need much – just a round, or maybe even half a round here and there.

- **Work in waves:** Follow a short sequence with a longer one and then follow that with an ultra-short one. Sounds tricky, but it isn't. It's just a question of dynamics and balance. If you spend a long time doing the same thing, it's time to change the technique, sequence or yarn. Let things come and go in waves.

- **Colourful auxiliary yarns:** I very often use two contrasting colours as auxiliary yarns as it adds a certain wildness and pushes the boundaries of beauty. Fuchsia pink and lime green are always a safe bet. Colourful auxiliaries will make the eye curious – like, what the hell's going on here?

- **Repetition:** Try knitting a sequence and then repeating it a few stripes later. It looks great! Like, what's going on now? But the overall effect is calming.

- **Crisis time:** If you find yourself in crisis, go back to something safe. Knit with your base colours or repeat a colour sequence you know will work!

KNIT IDENTICAL PIECES LIKE SLEEVES AT THE SAME TIME

- To knit two identical pieces – such as sleeves – knit them simultaneously. That's what I do, even when I'm using the Bad Idea Scrap technique. I alternate between one sleeve and the other. That way I know they'll turn out more or less the same.
  PS: They don't have to be identical.

𝕮𝖍𝖆𝖕𝖙𝖊𝖗 5
Knitting Patterns*
(3 patterns)

*Here come my designs. New or not to knitting, Scrap techniques, knotting or multi-colour, just jump right in, feet first! The first patterns are simple and quite straightforward. But as you knit, try to do something that makes you a bit unsure, something you wouldn't normally do. Try something completely new.
Unless otherwise stated, you can knit most of my patterns in any of the three Scrap techniques: ATS, All Over or Bad Idea. But do stick to the suggested techniques, otherwise things could get ugly …

"Scrunchies, easy peasy cushions and the patchwork blanket that really does last forever."

The Scrap Scrunchie

You can knit this in one colour or use one of the three Scrap techniques.

One colour	Knit with 2 strands of basic yarn.
ATS (p. 102)	Knit with 2 strands of basic yarn and inserted scrap strands.
All Over (p. 106)	Knit with 1 strand of basic yarn and 1 scrap strand all over.
Bad Idea (p. 110)	Knit with either 1, 2 or 3 scrap strands in order to get the right tension. You will need to knit a tension square (p. 44).
Basic yarn	e.g. Merino Cotton or Superwash Vital (50 g = 120 m/115 m), Silk Kid Mohair (25 g = 210 m) (p. 263, Yarn Types and Alternatives).
Scrap yarn	Shorter or longer strands for ATS. Knotted balls/skeins for All Over. Scrap yarn in all shades for Bad Idea (p. 97, Scrap yarn).
Size	Approx. 19 cm diameter.
Yarn requirements	Just under 2 balls of yarn per scrunchie (more on this in the instructions on p. 130) + at least 20 g scrap yarn (p. 260, Yarn Requirements).
Needles	Circular needle size 6 (60 cm), crochet hook size 5 to crochet the edges together.
Accessories	Hair tie to suit your hair. I like the cheap, soft ones best because my hair is thin and fine and feathery.
Tension square	Approx. 15 stitches and 22 rows of stocking stitch with size 6 needles = 10 x 10 cm (p. 44 Tension Squares). If your tension square is bigger, try thinner needles. If it's smaller, try thicker ones.

The Scrap Scrunchie is a good, fun project for beginners. It's great practice at casting on (p. 22), knitting stocking stitch in rounds (p. 33) and crocheting edges together with slip stitch (p. 49). It's knitted following a basic pattern, which you can combine with whatever Scrap techniques you like. If you're an experienced knitter and want to try out a Scrap technique, now's your chance. Just cast on 100 stitches and knit 30 rounds.

Knitting a scrunchie gives you a thousand opportunities to really let rip. You knit it on a circular needle, so it comes out as a tube. You then crochet the top and bottom edges of the tube together round the hair tie. Follow the basic pattern and with your favourite Scrap technique.

>

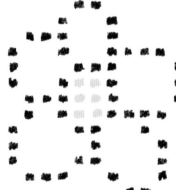

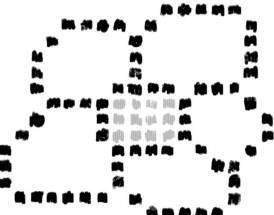

One colour.

ATS (p. 102).

All Over (p. 106).

Bad Idea (p. 110).

You could try and sketch your Scrunchie design first. You'll find my cool drawing tips on page 87.

Basic pattern
THE SCRAP SCRUNCHIE

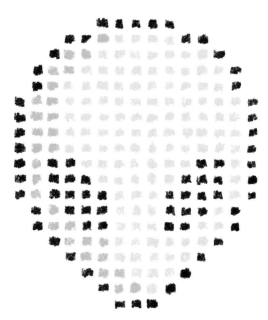

Follow the exact instructions for the scrunchie using your chosen Scrap technique. Cast on 100 stitches with a size 6 circular needle, join both ends to form a circle and knit 30 rounds of stocking stitch. Your knitting will roll up, but don't worry, that's normal. And it doesn't matter if you knit 28 or 31 rounds either. On the last round, cast off, but not too tightly. Stitch (p. 65) or knot any loose ends (p. 101). Now fold the scrunchie over to form a tunnel for your hair tie. Insert the hair tie and crochet the open edges together. Crochet through the two outer loops of the stitches (p. 49). Slowly push your hair tie further along as you go. Crochet the edges together all the way round and then stitch or knot the loose ends. The crocheted edge will end up around the outside and give your scrunchie a nice finish.

This is how you use the various Scrap techniques

ATS

The basic yarn is something like 1 ball Merino Cotton or Superwash Vital, and you are knitting it with 1 ball Silk Kid Mohair plus scrap strands of various lengths. Follow the basic pattern, knitting with two strands together: e.g. 1 strand Silk Kid Mohair + 1 strand Merino Cotton – or whatever basic yarn you've chosen. Knit as described in the ATS introduction (p. 102) and include as many or as few scrap strands as you like. Personally, I think it looks nicest if you cut off the mohair strand and then knot it in again to resume. That way it will come to the fore as an auxiliary yarn alongside your basic yarn.

Keep the basic strand running throughout. Choose two colours that go well together. Alternatively, for a funkier look, use two completely different-coloured strands.

All Over

The basic yarn is 1 ball Silk Kid Mohair, for example, which you are knitting with 1 strand of All Over scrap yarn that you've wound into balls/skeins. Knit the two strands together, following the basic pattern. When casting on and off, don't use a scrap yarn that's too thick or thin as it won't look good. Use the thick and thin yarns for the rest of the scrunchie instead. Try out different colour combinations. The result will look different every time.

Bad Idea

You can use any type of basic yarn for this, but experiment a bit first to get the right tension. Use different thicknesses of yarn and adjust your tension as you knit different thicknesses of strand together. That way you'll develop a feel for the personality and characteristics of the yarn. Follow the basic pattern using two or three strands at a time. And you're the boss, so you can change colour and yarn whenever you like.

Scrunchies are ideal for testing whether the different Scrap techniques suit your character and style.

Pattern
The Easy Peasy Pillow

You can knit this in one colour or use one of the three Scrap techniques.

One colour	Knit with 5 strands of basic yarn.
ATS (p. 102)	Knit with 5 strands of basic yarn and inserted scrap strands.
All Over (p. 106)	Knit with 4 strands of basic yarn and 1 scrap strand All Over.
Bad Idea (p. 110)	Knit with 1, 2, 3, 4, 5 or 6 strands to get the right tension. You will need to knit a tension square (p. 44).
Basic yarn	e.g. Merino Cotton or Superwash Vital (50 g = 120 m/115 m) (p. 263, Yarn Types and Alternatives).
Scrap yarn	Shorter or longer strands for ATS. Knotted balls/skeins for All Over. Scrap yarn in all colour shades for Bad Idea (p. 97, Scrap Yarn).
Size	Approx. 40 x 40 (50 x 50) cm after putting the cover on.

Yarn requirements

ATS	9 (10) balls Superwash Vital or Merino Cotton + at least 100 g scrap yarn.
All Over	8 (9) balls Superwash Vital or Merino Cotton + at least 100 g scrap yarn.
Bad Idea	Approx. 400 (500) g scrap yarn (p. 260, Yarn Requirements).
Needles	Circular needle size 10 (80 cm), crochet hook size 6 to crochet the edges together.
Accessories	Cushion, 40 x 40 or 50 x 50 cm.
Tension square	9-10 stitches and 16 rows stocking stitch on size 10 needles = 10 x 10 cm before putting the cover on (p. 44, Tension Squares). If your tension square is bigger, try thinner needles. If it's smaller, try thicker ones.

"Cushions? *No way!*" you're probably thinking. I hear you! That's exactly what I thought when some of my friends suggested I include them in my book. At Design School the teachers were constantly waffling on about cushions and cushion design here, there and everywhere. I just thought: "Whaaat? I'm not designing a cushion. Not cool. Not sexy." And what was the very first design I ever sold? A cushion, of course! As a design student I was against cushions in general, but there are times when a good cushion really doesn't go amiss.

Either way, I had a lot of fun creating these cushions for you, and if I may say so myself, they really are absolutely awesome! Cushions are easy to knit, so they're good for beginners, but they're great fun for experienced knitters too.

Follow the pattern and choose a design and colours that suit your home and mood.

>

Embroidery (p. 186) on the cushions is supercool. Cushion knitted in stocking stitch in the All Over Scrap technique (p. 106).

Single rib pattern in ATS (p. 102).

Ombré stocking stitch in All Over (p. 106).

Wide rib pattern in All Over (p. 106).

Checks in ATS (p. 102).

The Easy Peasy Pillow knitted in stocking stitch and ombré with a basic colour scheme of light blue and white. Knitted in the All Over Scrap technique (p. 106).

Basic pattern
THE EASY PEASY PILLOW

Cast on 72 (90) stitches on a size 10 circular needle. Join both ends to form a circle and mark the beginning of the round. Knit 50 (60) rounds in your chosen design: stocking stitch, single rib, double rib, checks, ombré, stripes or whatever you like. You can slip the cushion in if you like, to see if your cover is a few centimetres smaller than the cushion, as it should be. If not, just knit or unravel a few rounds (p. 64) until you get the right size. In the last round, cast off the stitches using plain knitting. Slip the cushion into the cover and carefully crochet the edges together along one side using slip stitch (p. 49). Insert the crochet hook only through the outer loops, otherwise the seam will be too thick. Then darn in the ends. Crochet the edges on the other side together in the same way, with the cushion inside. Do it as neatly as you can! Darn in the ends or knot them together (p. 100). Make sure you keep the cushion cover nice and flat while you're crocheting so that the stitches match up. Don't rush it. Darn in the last ends and pull them through from the right side to the wrong side, twice. Darn in the strands on the front last, pull them fairly tight and cut them off. Then they will disappear into the knitting. Or… just do it whatever way you like!

Different patterns

Stocking stitch

Follow the pattern and the instructions for your chosen Scrap technique. Work every round in plain knitting (the result will look like stocking stitch because you're knitting in rounds). You can use either side of your knitting as the right side. It's your cushion, so it's your choice.

Single rib pattern

Follow the pattern and the instructions for your chosen Scrap technique.

Knit in single twisted rib (k1 tbl, p1 to the end of the round; repeat). Continue knitting in rounds until your work is long enough. To make a neat edge that you can crochet together, cast off all stitches in the last round using plain knit stitch.

Make sure the stitches match up exactly on both sides while you're crocheting them together.

Ombré stocking stitch

The ombré cushion can only be knitted in All Over. Use two different colours of basic yarn (A and B) for the colour gradient. Follow the basic pattern. Cast on with 4 strands of A plus 1 scrap strand (5 strands altogether). Knit 7 (9) rounds. Replace 1 strand of A with 1 strand of B so you have 3 strands of A, 1 strand of B plus 1 scrap strand. Knit 6 (7) rounds. Replace the next strand of A with 1 strand of B so you have 2 strands of A and 2 strands of B plus 1 scrap strand. Knit 6 (7) rounds. Replace the next strand of A with 1 strand of B so you've 1 strand of A, 3 strands of B plus 1 scrap strand. Knit 6 (7) rounds. Replace your last strand of A with 1 strand of B. You now have 4 strands of B plus 1 scrap strand. Continue in stocking stitch (i.e. knitting every round in plain knitting on the circular needle) until you've knitted a total of 50 (60) rounds. Continue by following the basic pattern. If you prefer to have the "wrong" side on the outside, be sure to darn in the strands on the "right" side.

Wide rib pattern

Follow the pattern and the introduction to your chosen Scrap technique.

Cast on and knit in wide rib (40 x 40 cm: k6, p6, repeat) (50 x 50 cm: k5, p5, repeat) to the end of the round. Keep on knitting until your work is long enough. To make a neat edge that you can crochet together, cast off all stitches in the last round using plain knit stitch.

Before crocheting the edges together, insert the cushion and pull the cover into place so that the stitches match up properly top and bottom – knit stitches opposite knit stitches and purls opposite purls. Otherwise it will look very ugly.

Check pattern

Follow the pattern and the instructions in the introduction to your chosen Scrap technique.

Cast on and knit in wide rib (40 x 40 cm: k6, p6, repeat) (50 x 50 cm: k5, p5, repeat) to the end of the round. Knit 10 rounds and then reverse the pattern (40 x 40 cm: p6, k6 , repeat) (50 x 50 cm: p5, k5, repeat), so you're now knitting a row of purl above plain knit and vice versa. Knit to the end of the round. After 10 rounds of this sequence, switch back to the first variant. This will produce a square check pattern. Keep changing after every 10 rounds until you've knitted 50 (60) rounds.

To make a neat edge that you can crochet together, cast off all stitches in the last round using plain knit stitch.

When you crochet the ends together, the squares should match up. Whether plain knitting meets plain or purl doesn't matter, but make sure the actual squares match up neatly. It's easiest if you pull the cover straight before crocheting, after inserting the cushion.

Carefully crocheting the edges together using slip stitch (p. 49).

Pattern
The Bad Idea Blanket

You can only knit this using the Bad Idea technique.

Bad Idea (p. 110)	Knit with 1, 2 or, 3 strands to get the right tension. You'll need to knit a tension square (p. 44).
Basic yarn	e. g. Merino Cotton or Superwash Vital (50 g = 120 m/115 m) for the edges (p. 263, Yarn Types and Alternatives).
Scrap yarn	Scrap yarn in all different colours and shades for Bad Idea (p. 97, Scrap Yarn).
Size	Approx. 180 x 140 cm – or whatever. It depends on how many stripes you knit and how long they are.
Yarn requirements	Approx. 4 balls basic yarn for edges and finishing + at least 1,500 g scrap yarn (p. 260, Yarn Requirements).
Needles	Knitting needles size 4 and crochet hook size 3.5 for assembly and edging.
Accessories	Patience, time, a good mood and lots of nibbles to keep you going.
Tension square	19-20 stitches and 35 rows of garter stitch with size 4 needles = 10 x 10 cm. A tension square isn't essential, but if you knit with lots of different yarns, all the squares in the blanket will turn out different sizes (p. 44, Tension Squares). If your tension square is bigger, try thinner needles. If it's smaller, try thicker ones.

This is the simplest blanket in the world. It'll take you 100 years to knit it, but it is really megafantastic and awesome. It's knitted in garter stitch and consists of at least five separate strips (the equivalent of five scarves). These are all knitted in different yarns to make stripes of varying width and length using the Bad Idea technique (p. 110). You then crochet around the edges of them in slip stitch (p. 49) – preferably in a quieter colour such as white, black or grey. If you're a beginner, don't choose black: it's horrible to crochet because you can hardly see the stitches. Knitting different widths and lengths of stripe is great too because it ends up with a patchwork effect. But if you're a control freak and the whole idea gives you the creeps, just knit strips that are the same width and length. Whatever you do, make sure the edge stitches are neat (p. 37), because it will make it easier to crochet around and assemble the strips.

By the way, the strips also make very smart scarves – just in case you start regretting your decision to make the blanket halfway through. That can happen! Once, I spent ages working on a blanket – collecting wool and then knitting whenever I had nothing else going on or had got frustrated or bored with my main knitting project.

Choose the colours for your blanket according to the various guidelines for the Bad Idea technique. When you're knitting such a large item it can make sense to buy/ swap/find some colours/yarns so you have between three and five different ones. You can then use them as your basic yarn. In other words, you'll knit various sections in every strip in these basic colours. It will give the blanket more calmness and continuity and make it look less crazy.

>

The Bad Idea Blanket looks great when it's
finished. You can use the same basic yarn to
crochet round and assemble the strips.

Basic pattern
The Bad Idea Blanket

Cast on between 35 and 60 stitches using size 4 needles and knit rows of garter stitch. Use the BUTT (p. 37) for your edge stitches. Work in the Bad Idea technique and keep on knitting. When your work is long enough, e.g. 165–180 cm, cast off. Put your 1st strip to one side and knit another one, which could be a different width and length – or the same, if you prefer. You'll need to make at least five strips, but six would be better if you can manage. When you've finished all your strips, take one and start crocheting around the edge. Start anywhere along one of the long sides and use a size 3.5 crochet hook to do slip stitch all the way round, inserting your crochet hook through both loops of the BUTT (p. 49). At the corners, crochet 2–3 slip stitches into the same hole to make a nice rounded corner. Do the same with the other strips. Darn in or knot the ends of the yarn (p. 100). Lay out all strips on the floor – keep any crawling kiddies well away – and mark the middle of the 1st strip with a book, or similar. Put the next one beside it so that the middle of the strips match up. Arrange all the strips in whatever way you think looks best. Alternate between longer and shorter strips, or between wider and narrower ones for a more harmonious look. Take time over arranging the strips so they look good together. (If only you knew how much time designers spend arranging and then rearranging things!) When you're satisfied, take a photo to remind yourself what goes where. Now start to assemble the blanket. Starting on a long edge at one end of the blanket, crochet two strips together using slip stitch.

Insert your crochet hook through the slip stitches. Do this all the way along edges until you reach the end. Cut off the yarn. Start at the same end of the blanket as before and add the next strip. Crochet it together with the two strips that you have already joined together. Continue until you have crocheted all the strips together to make a blanket, then darn in or knot the ends of the yarn.

HOW TO GET ALL THE SEAMS TO LIE THE SAME WAY

- The blanket will look best if you always start at the same end when you're crocheting the pieces together. That way all the seams will lie in the same direction. If you really love crocheting, you can turn the blanket over and slip-stitch all the strips together on the other side as well, using the upper loops of the BUTT. It will look awesome and will really impress your mother. But that's not essential, of course. I've never actually done that myself as I'm far too lazy!

Chapter 6
Knitting Patterns*
(3 patterns)

"The only kiddies' cardigan you will ever need in this life, a standard child's pullover on tiny needles that's actually not the least bit standard, and Lulu's cute little sweater dress."

Pattern
The Larseman Cardigan

You can knit this in one colour or use one of the three Scrap techniques.

For kids I always knit one or two sizes bigger than they actually need. That way you can always use the pullover as a dress – or even a doll's blanket!

One colour	Knit with 2 strands of basic yarn.
ATS (p. 102)	Knit with 2 strands of basic yarn and inserted scrap strands.
All Over (p. 106)	Knit with 1 strand of basic yarn and 1 scrap strand all over.
Bad Idea (p. 110)	Knit with 1, 2 or 3 scrap strands to get the right tension. You'll need to knit a tension square (p. 44).
Basic yarn	e.g. Extrafine Merino 150 (50 g = 150 m) (p. 263, Yarn Types and Alternatives)
Scrap yarn	Shorter or longer strands for ATS. Knotted balls/skeins for All Over. Scrap yarn in all colours and shades for Bad Idea (p. 97, Scrap Yarn).
Size	6–12 months (2 years) 4 years (6 years)
Chest measurement of the garment	Approx. 62 (66) 74 (78) cm. Overall chest measurement, measured directly under the armholes on the knitting (p. 66, Sizes).
Overall length	Approx. 27 (30) 34 (37) cm from shoulder to bottom edge.

Yarn requirements

One colour	Approx. 6 (7) 8 (10) balls Extrafine Merino.
ATS	Approx. 5 (6) 7 (9) balls Extrafine Merino + at least 50 g scrap yarn.
All Over	Approx. 3 (3) 4 (5) balls Extrafine Merino + at least 150 g scrap yarn.
Bad Idea	Approx. 250 (300) 350 (450) g scrap yarn (p. 260, Yarn Requirements).
Needles	Circular needle size 5 (80 cm, for body and yoke), double-pointed needles size 5 (for sleeves, unless you knit with *Magic Loop*), crochet hook size 5 (to close sleeves seams and attach sleeve), crochet hook size 4 (to crochet around edges, if desired).
Tension square	18 stitches and 33–34 rows with two strands in garter stitch on size 5 needles = 10 x 10 cm (p. 44, Tension Square). If your tension square is bigger, try thinner needles. If it's smaller, try thicker ones.

A truly cute child's cardy which both my kids have in many different variations. The speckled look, different yarn scraps and coarseness of the garter stitch ribs are awesome. Also, it's the perfect cardigan for your offspring because they can spatter spaghetti, tomato sauce and pureed vegetables all over it and nobody will notice. The stains just blend in with the colours of the cardy – so there's no need to worry about your beautiful knitting being ruined. But do remember to wash it before it gets beyond disgusting.

"Hey! Where the hell are the sizes for 8 to 10 years?", I hear you ask. Well, in my experience, kids that age don't want to wear hand-knitted cardigans any more. Sadly...

The Larseman Cardigan is knitted with two strands of yarn in plain knitting (garter stitch). It's knitted from bottom to top in rows, on a circular needle. That means the two fronts and the back are all worked in a single piece. The sleeves can be turned back a bit, and there are no buttonholes because the knitting is so loose you can pull a button through without a proper buttonhole. It's up to you how many buttons you want.

Knit the BUTT (p. 37) in the first stitch and knit the last stitch of every row in plain knitting. That will produce a nice edge that's easy to crochet together. On the sleeves you'll increase alternately on every 4th or 6th row. That means you knit 3 rows and increase on the 4th row, then knit 5 rows and increase on the 6th. After that you go back to knitting 3 rows followed by an increase on the 4th, and so on. That will produce the nicest rounding on the sleeve in the few centimetres that are available to knit. You can decide yourself whether to crochet a row around the front edges and the neckline in slip stitch (p. 49) or not. The cardy looks cute with or without.

>

ATS (p. 102).

Bad Idea (p. 110).

All Over (p. 106).

All Over with a dark base (p. 106).

All Over with
scrap yarn in
muted colours.

Basic pattern
THE LARSEMAN CARDIGAN

Back and fronts

Cast on 111 (118) 131 (142) stitches with circular needle size 5 and knit rows of plain knitting (garter stitch). After 29 (31) 34 (37), stitches set a marker for the right front. Knit 53 (56) 63 (68) stitches and set another marker = back. Knit the last 29 (31) 34 (37) stitches = left front. Continue knitting in garter stitch, with the BUTT at beginning of every row. Continue until the knitting reaches 14 (15) 18 (21) cm. In the next row cast off 2 (2) 3 (3) stitches on either side of the two markers. 103 (110) 119 (130) stitches remain. Put your knitting to one side – either on another needle or on a length of yarn.

Sleeves (both the same)

Cast on 29 (31) 33 (35) stitches with circular needle size 5. Knit 4 cm in plain knitting (garter stitch) for the cuff. Don't forget the BUTT (p. 37). Continue knitting in garter stitch, increasing 1 stitch at beginning and end of every 4th and then every 6th row alternately until you've added a total of 8 (10) 11 (14) stitches on each side (= 45 (51) 55 (63) stitches). Increase as follows: BUTT on the 1st stitch, k1, inc1, knit to last 2 stitches, inc1, k2. Continue until the sleeve is 18 (21) 24 (27) cm long. At beginning of next 2 rows, cast off 2 (2) 3 (3) stitches for the armholes = 41 (47) 49 (57) stitches. Put the work to one side and knit the 2nd sleeve in the same way.

Yoke

Place all sections on circular needle size 5 with the right side of the knitting outside, setting the sleeves above the armholes on the back and fronts. It is important to ensure that the right side is outermost, otherwise there will be an ugly groove of stocking stitch. The sleeves are correctly positioned when the end of the cut-off strand on the last row you knitted is on the right-hand side – then the right side will be facing outwards. With the inside of the left front facing you, BUTT the first stitch as your edge stitch and knit one row of plain knitting. Set a marker for each transition between the different pieces: between left front and left sleeve, between left sleeve and back, between back and right sleeve, and between right sleeve and right front = a total of 4 markers.

In the next row decrease for the raglan on the armhole side of the front of the cardy. To do this, *knit in plain knitting (garter stitch) until 3 stitches before the marker, dec 1 (sl1 k1 psso) (p. 61), k1. Slip the marker from the left-hand needle to the right-hand needle, then k1, dec 1 (k2tog) (p. 61)*, repeat from * to end. Repeat this on every 2nd row.

Knit a total of 12 (13) 15 (16) rows with a raglan decrease (= 24 (26) 30 (32) rows altogether). Continuing the raglan decreases as before, but in the next 2 rows cast off 4 (5) 6 (7) stitches at beginning of row for the neck as well. Do this as follows:

Cast off 4 (5) 6 (7) stitches, knit to end of row. Cast off 4 (5) 6 (7) stitches at beginning of next row – incorporating raglan decreases as you go.

At beginning of next 4 rows decrease 1 (1) 2 (2) stitches. In other words, dec1 (1) 2 (2), knit in garter stitch (plain knitting) to the end of the row, turn, dec1 (1) 2 (2), knit in garter stitch (plain knitting) to the end of the row, turn, etc., a total of 4 times. Continue to decrease for the raglan until 2 stitches remain before the markers on the front pieces. Cast off all remaining stitches with the right side facing you.

Finishing, edges and buttons

Crochet the sleeves seams together using a double strand of basic yarn and a size 5 crochet hook, working in slip stitch (p. 49) on the right side of the garment. Work on one sleeve from the armhole down to the cuff, and on the other from the cuff up to the armhole. That way the seams will look the same. Insert the crochet hook through the outer loops of the stitches as that will look neatest and the seams won't be too thick. Turn the sleeves and jacket inside out, crochet the holes under the arms together, also using slip stitch (p. 58), and darn in the ends. Fold the cuffs back and stitch in place with a few stitches if you like.

The front edges and neckline can stay as they are, or you can crochet round them if you prefer. To do this, use a size 4 crochet hook and two strands of basic yarn. Start on the lower part of the left front and crochet 1 slip stitch in each BUTT or stitch along the left edge. Work from bottom to top, then round the neck edge and along the right front edge from top to bottom. Insert the crochet hook through both loops or just the outer loop – that's up to you. Crochet 2-3 slip stitches into the same stitch on the corners to make a nice round edge. Cut off the yarn and either darn in the ends or knot them (p. 100). Sew on however many buttons you wish at a suitable distance (e.g. 3 cm) along the front.

Once, when I was casting on to knit this cardy, I didn't pay attention and ended up with four stitches too many on one of the fronts. I only noticed when I was casting off and couldn't be bothered to correct it. But the end result still looks pretty cool. Just so you know that not even that really matters!

151

The Not So Basic Kids' Sweater

You can knit this in one colour or use one of the three Scrap techniques.

One colour	Knit with 1 strand of basic yarn.
ATS (p. 102)	Knit with 1 strand of basic yarn and scrap strands inserted.
All Over (p. 106)	Knit stripes with 1 strand basic yarn and stripes with 1 strand scrap yarn all over. Knit all cuffs and neckline with basic yarn.
Bad Idea (p. 110)	Knit with 1, 2 or 3 scrap strands to get the right tension. You will need to knit a tension square (p. 44).

Basic yarn	e.g. Extrafine Merino 150 (50 g = 150 m) (p. 263, Yarn Types and Alternatives)
Scrap yarn	Shorter or longer strands for ATS. Knotted balls/skeins for All Over. Scrap yarn in all colours and shades for Bad Idea (p. 97, Scrap Yarn).
Size	2 (4) 6 (8) 10 years
Chest measurement of the garment	Approx. 66 (71) 77 (82) 87 cm. Overall chest measurement, measured directly under armholes on knitting (p. 66, Sizes).
Overall length	Approx. 34 (38) 42 (46) 50 cm from the shoulder to the bottom edge.

Yarn requirements

One colour	5 (6) 7 (8) 9 balls Extrafine Merino.
ATS	Approx. 4 (5) 6 (7) 8 balls Extrafine Merino plus at least 50 g scrap yarn.
All Over	Approx. 3 (3) 4 (5) 6 balls Extrafine Merino plus at least 150 g scrap yarn.
Bad Idea	Approx. 200 (250) 300 (350) 400 g scrap yarn (p. 260, Yarn Requirements).

Needles	Circular needle size 3.5 (60 cm, for front, back + yoke), double-pointed needles size 3.5 (for sleeves, unless you knit with *Magic Loop*), circular needle size 3 (60 cm, for cuffs and neck edging), double-pointed needles size 3 (for cuffs, unless you knit with *Magic Loop*), crochet hook size 3 (to crochet pieces together).
Tension square	Approx. 24 stitches and 33-34 rows of garter stitch on size 3.5 needles = 10 x 10 cm (p. 44, Tension Square). If your tension square is bigger, try thinner needles. If it's smaller, try thicker ones.

This is a really cute children's pullover. It's knitted with a single strand of yarn from bottom to top. You can make it in any of the three Scrap techniques. I knitted this pullover with only scrap yarn and size 2.5 to 3.5 needles – fairly fine needles and thin yarn, in other words. That way you'll end up with an awesome, nicely balanced knitted pullover without too many knots and irregularities. Remember: the sleeves will look a bit different because you'll have fewer stitches on each round, so the coloured stripes won't match up with the ones on the body. No worries, though. It'll still look very cute.

When I write that you can only knit the All Over version with stripes, it's because I don't think it will look good if you knit the whole thing with one strand All Over. The design needs to look less busy, so it's best to knit stripes of basic yarn. You can also knit the pullover in a single colour, of course. In fact, this is a pretty good pattern for a raglan pullover, even if I say it myself.

>

KNITTING STRIPES WITH THE ALL OVER TECHNIQUE

- To knit stripes, all you need to do is switch between your basic and scrap yarns. And instead of cutting off the yarn every time you change colour, just let the yarn you're not using dangle while you carry on knitting with the other yarn, your working yarn. When you're ready, take up the inactive yarn again and use it to knit the next stripe. When you switch between colours, don't pull the yarn too tight – it'll look horrible! Just loosely incorporate the inactive yarn along the side of your knitting while you carry on working with the active one. This will save you having to darn in or knot lots of yarn ends when you finish. You can also use this method to knit stripey socks (p. 214).

Bad Idea (p. 110).

ATS (p. 102).

All Over (p. 106).

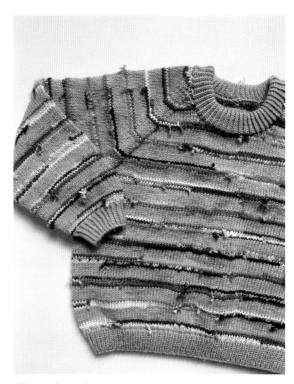

All Over (p. 106).

<u>One colour version
with embroidered
flowers (p. 186).</u>

Basic pattern
The Not So Basic Kid's Sweater

Striped pattern in All Over
4 rounds stocking stitch with scrap yarn
6 rounds stocking stitch with basic yarn
Repeat

Front and back
    Cast on 158 (170) 186 (198) 210 stitches with circular needle size 3. Join up the stitches to make a circle and mark the beginning of the round, which is the 1st side of the pullover. On the 1st round, knit 79 (85) 93 (99) 105 stitches in twisted rib (k1 tbl, p1, repeat), then set a marker for the other side of the pullover and continue to the end of the round. Knit 8 (10) 12 (12) 14 rounds in twisted rib. Switch to circular needle size 3.5 and continue in stocking stitch. If you're knitting All Over, start the stripe pattern here. If you're knitting ATS, Bad Idea or a single-colour pullover, simply continue in stocking stitch. Repeat the stripe pattern 5 (6) 7 (8) 9 times. On the last round (= 6th round with basic yarn) cast off 3 (3) 4 (5) 5 stitches for the armholes on both sides of the markers. If you're knitting ATS, Bad Idea or single-colour, continue knitting until your work measures approx. 16 (19) 21 (25) 29 cm from the top of the rib section, then cast off for the armholes as described above. Put your work to one side.

Sleeves (both the same)
    Cast on 42 (44) 46 (48) 50 stitches with double-pointed needles or circular needle size 3 and Magic Loop (p. 41). Join up the stitches to make a circle and mark the beginning of the round. Knit for 10 (12) 12 (14) 16 rounds in twisted rib (k1 tbl, p1, repeat). Change to double-pointed needles size 3.5 (or circular needle size 3.5 and Magic Loop). Knit in stocking stitch and start the stripe pattern – but only if you're knitting All Over. For ATS, Bad Idea or single-colour continue with that. In the 1st round, increase evenly along the round until you have 48 (50) 52 (52)

56 stitches. Continue in stocking stitch. On the 5th round, above the cuff, increase 1 stitch on each side of the marker (p. 61). To do this, k2, inc 1, continue knitting in stocking stitch to the last 2 stitches, inc 1, k2. Repeat on every 5th round 10 (12) 13 (15) 16 times = 68 (74) 78 (82) 88 stitches. Repeat the striped pattern 7 (8) 9 (10) 11 times (after the cuff and only for All Over). In the last round of the last stripe (= 6th round with basic yarn), cast off 3 (3) 4 (5) 5 stitches for the armholes on both sides of the markers. If you're knitting ATS, Bad Idea or single-colour, continue until your work measures approx. 22 (25) 28 (32) 35 cm from the top of the rib section. Cast off for the armholes as described above. Put your work to one side and knit the 2nd sleeve in the same way.

Yoke
    Place all sections on circular needle size 3.5, setting the sleeves above the armholes on the back and front. Place a marker between the right sleeve and the back – that is the sleeve to your right when you lay the knitting flat on the table with the back uppermost – this is the start of each round. Continue the stripe pattern – or ATS, Bad Idea or your single colour – by knitting 1 round in stocking stitch, setting a marker for each transition between the different pieces for the yoke – 4 markers in total. In the next row, decrease for the raglan: * k1, k2 tog (p. 61), continue in stocking stitch until 3 stitches before the marker, dec 1 (sl1 k1 psso) (p. 61), k1*. Slip the marker from the left-hand needle to the right-hand needle, repeat from * to end. Repeat on every 2nd row. Continue raglan decrease until 47 (49) 51 (53) 55 stitches remain on the yoke front. The next round you knit should be a row without decreases. Cast off the middle 13 (15) 17 (19) 21 stitches for the neck opening, knit to end of round. Cut off the yarn.

Slide all the stitches from one needle to the other without knitting them. Now start the neck opening on the left side of the knitting and the right side of your work – that is, the side on your left when you lay the knitting with the front uppermost flat on the table. Now knit stocking stitch in rows.

    Cast off for the neck opening while continuing the raglan decrease. Continue the stripe pattern, ATS, Bad Idea or your single colour from wherever you left off. For the neck opening, cast off 2 stitches at beginning of row and knit to the end. In the next row, cast off 2 stitches at beginning of row and purl to the end. Remember the BUTT for the edges, as it will be easier to pick up the stitches for the neckband later on. In the next 6 rows, cast off 1 stitch at beginning of each row. Continue in stocking stitch in rows, with the raglan decreases as before on the right side of your work until 2 stitches remain before the markers on the front pieces. Cast off all remaining stitches on the right side.

Finishing and neckband
    Sew or crochet the armholes together inside the work. Darn in or knot all yarn ends (p. 100). Starting in the middle of the back, with the right side of the work facing you (p. 56), use a size 3 circular needle to pick up 9 stitches for every 10 stitches around the neck opening. Make sure you end up with an even number of stitches. Then knit 5 cm in twisted rib (k1 tbl, p1). Cast off loosely. Fold over the neckband into the pullover and crochet it down with slip stitch (p. 49) – or loosely stitch it into place.

The No Limits Sweaters in partner look knitted using the Bad Idea Scrap technique. Instructions on p. 166.

Pattern
The Lulu Sweater Dress

You can knit this in a single colour or use one of the three Scrap techniques.

One colour	Knit with 1 strand basic yarn.
ATS (p. 102)	Knit with 1 strand basic yarn and inserted scrap strands.
All Over (p. 106)	Knit stripes with 1 strand basic yarn and stripes with 1 strand scrap yarn all over. Knit cuffs and neckline with basic yarn.
Bad Idea (p. 110)	Knit with 1, 2 or 3 scrap strands to get the right tension. You will need to knit a tension square (p. 44).

Basic yarn	e.g. Extrafine Merino 150 (50 g = 150 m) (p. 263, Yarn Types and Alternatives)
Scrap yarn	Shorter or longer strands for ATS. Knotted balls/skeins for All Over. Scrap yarn in all colours and shades for Bad Idea (p. 97, Scrap Yarn).
Size	2 (4) 6 (8) 10 years
Chest measurement of the garment	Approx. 66 (71) 77 (82) 87 cm. Overall chest measurement, measured directly under armholes on knitting (p. 66, Sizes).
Overall length	Approx. 48 (54) 60 (64) 68 cm from shoulder to bottom edge.

Yarn requirements

One colour	Approx. 7 (7) 8 (9) 10 balls Extrafine Merino.
ATS	Approx. 6 (6) 7 (8) 9 balls Extrafine Merino + at least 80 g scrap yarn.
All Over	AApprox. 4 (4) 5 (6) 7 balls Extrafine Merino + at least 175 g scrap yarn.
Bad Idea	Approx. 300 (300) 350 (400) 450 g of scrap yarn (p. 260, Yarn Requirements).

Needles	Circular needle size 3.5 (60 cm; for front, back + yoke), double-pointed needles size 3.5 (for the sleeves, unless you knit with *Magic Loop*), circular needle size 3 (60 cm for cuffs and neck edging), double-pointed needles size 3 (for the sleeve cuffs, unless you knit with *Magic Loop*), crochet hook size 3 (to crochet pieces together).
Tension square	Approx. 24 stitches and 33-34 rows garter stitch on size 3.5 needles = 10 x 10 cm (p. 44, Tension Squares). If your tension square is bigger, try thinner needles. If it's smaller, try thicker ones.

Dresses are a sort of baptism of fire when it comes to knitting in the round, because you have so many stitches on your needles. That is why I almost always opt for dresses with a skirt that begins at hip level – with a drop-waist, in other words. In this pattern, the skirt is really an extension of a long pullover. I simply can't be bothered to spend so long knitting rounds with so many stitches unless it's actually for me. Sorry, but that's the politically incorrect truth.

Well, whatever. This dress is knitted from bottom to top in any of the three Scrap techniques. But your scrap yarn should be suitable for needles sizes 2.5 to 3.5 so it doesn't turn out too bulky. Try a few different yarns in the right thickness. You'll soon work it out. If you don't like the look, just cut off the yarn and try something else. Don't forget: your knitting will look different on the sleeves from on the body because you have fewer stitches in each round.

The cuffs and edging (or 'welts' if you want to use the posh word for this!) on the dress are knitted in moss stitch and are not folded back and crocheted down. You could also knit the dress in a single colour, and perhaps finish it with embroidery (p. 186) or beads (p. 244) – if the recipient is lucky.

>

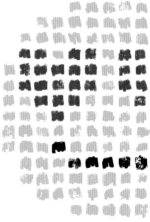

All Over (p. 106).

ATS (p. 102).

The Lulu Sweater Dress in All Over - but oops! The neckband is in the wrong stitch. Never mind. It can happen to anyone.

Basic pattern
The Lulu Sweater Dress

Stripe pattern in the All Over technique
4 rounds stocking stitch with scrap yarn
6 rounds stocking stitch with basic yarn
Repeat

Moss stitch
1st round: k1, p1, repeat to end of round
2nd round: p1, k1, repeat to end of round
Repeat these two rounds

Skirt section

Cast on 316 (340) 372 (396) 420 with circular needle size 3. Join up the stitches to make a circle and mark the end of the round. Knit rounds in moss stitch (see above). In the 1st round, set a marker after 158 (170) 186 (198) 210 stitches = other side of the dress. Continue knitting in moss stitch for a total of 4 (4) 6 (8) 8 rounds. Change over to circular needle size 3.5 and begin with stocking stitch and the stripe pattern – but only if you're knitting All Over. For ATS, Bad Idea or single-colour continue with that. Repeat the stripe pattern 3 (3) 4 (4) 5 times. Start a new repeat of the stripe pattern, and in the 4th round of the scrap yarn stripe, k2tog all the way to the end of the round. You will end up with only half as many stitches on the needle: 158 (170) 186 (198) 210 stitches. If you're knitting ATS, Bad Idea or in a single colour, knit until your work measures approx. 10 (10) 13 (13) 16 cm from the top of the moss-stitch section, then k2tog across the round as described above. Change to basic yarn if you're knitting stripes, otherwise continue with ATS, Bad Idea or a single colour. Knit 1 round in stocking stitch and then 6 rounds in moss stitch.

Front and back

Start with the 1st round of the stripe pattern – or continue with ATS, Bad Idea or a single colour. Repeat the stripe pattern 5 (6) 7 (8) 9 times. In the last round of the last repeat of the stripe pattern (= 6th round

with basic yarn), cast off 3 (3) 4 (5) 5 stitches for the armholes on both sides of the markers. If you're knitting ATS, Bad Idea or single-colour, continue knitting until your work measures approx. 16 (19) 21 (25) 29 cm from the top of the moss stitch section – from the top of the skirt, in other words. Then cast off for the armholes as described above. Put your work to one side.

Sleeves (both the same)

Cast on 42 (44) 46 (48) 50 stitches with double-pointed needles or circular needle size 3 and Magic Loop (p. 41). Mark the beginning of the round and join up the stitches to make a circle. Knit 10 (12) 12 (14) 16 rounds in moss stitch. Change to double-pointed needles size 3.5 (or circular needle size 3.5 and Magic Loop). Knit in stocking stitch and begin with the stripe pattern – but only if you're knitting All Over. For ATS, Bad Idea or single-colour continue with that. In the 1st round, increase evenly across the round until you have 48 (50) 52 (52) 56 stitches. Continue in stocking stitch. Five rounds above the cuff, increase 1 stitch on each side of the marker (p. 61) as follows: k2, inc 1, continue knitting in stocking stitch to the last 2 stitches, inc 1, k2. Increase as described in every 5th round a total of 10 (12) 13 (15) 16 times = 68 (74) 78 (82) 88 stitches. Repeat the striped pattern 7 (8) 9 (10) 11 times (after the cuff and only for All Over). In the last round of the last repeat of the stripe (= 6th round with basic yarn) cast off 3 (3) 4 (5) 5 stitches for the armholes on both sides of the markers. If you're knitting ATS, Bad Idea or single-colour, continue knitting until your work measures approx. 22 (25) 28 (32) 35 cm from the top of the rib section. Cast off for the armholes as described above. Put your work to one side and knit the 2nd sleeve in the same way.

Yoke

Place all sections on circular needle size 3.5, setting the sleeves above the armholes on the back and front. Place a marker between the right sleeve and the back – that is the sleeve to your right when you lay the knitting flat on the table with the back uppermost = the start of each round. Start the stripe pattern here again – or carry on with ATS, Bad Idea or your single colour. Knit 1 round in stocking stitch, setting a marker for each transition between the different pieces for the yoke = a total of 4 markers. In the next row, decrease for the raglan as follows: * k1, k2 tog (p. 61), continue in stocking stitch until 3 stitches before the marker, dec 1 (sl1 k1 psso) (p. 61), k1*. Slip the marker from the left-hand needle to the right-hand needle, repeat from * to end and repeat on every 2nd row. Continue to decrease for the raglan until 47 (49) 51 (53) 55 stitches remain on the yoke front. Your next round should be one without decreases. Next round: Cast off the middle 13 (15) 17 (19) 21 stitches for the neck opening, knit to end of round. Cut off the yarn. Slide all the stitches from one needle to the other without knitting them. Now you can begin the neck opening on the left side of the knitting and the right side of your work – that is, the side on your left when you lay the knitting with the front uppermost flat on the table. Now knit stocking stitch in rows.

Cast off for the neck opening and at the same time continue to knit the decreases for the raglan – continue with the stripe pattern from wherever you left off, or continue with ATS, Bad Idea or your single colour. For the neck opening cast off 2 stitches at beginning of next two rows as follows: cast off 2 stitches at beginning of row, knit

The dress is knitted in the ATS Scrap technique (p. 102) and with a basic yarn in white. Super-practical when eating spaghetti with tomato sauce!

to end of the row; in the next row, cast off 2 stitches at beginning of row and then purl to the end of the row.

Don't forget the BUTT for the edge stitches, as it makes it easier to pick up the stitches for the neck-band later on. In the next 6 rows, cast off one stitch at beginning of each row. Continue to knit stocking stitch in rows, with the raglan decreases as before on the right

side of your work, until 2 stitches remain before the markers on the front pieces. Cast off all remaining stitches with the right side of your work facing you.

Finishing and neck edging
With the dress inside out, sew or crochet the cast-off section of the sleeves onto the cast-off section of the armholes (p. 58), darn in or knot all yarn ends (p. 100). Now,

starting to work in the middle of the back, with the right side of the work facing you (p. 56), use a size 3 circular needle, pick up 9 stitches for every 10 stitches around the neck opening. Making sure that you end up with an even number of stitches. Knit 2.5 cm in moss stitch and then cast off in moss stitch by doing p1 over k1, k1 over p1, so that the moss-stitch pattern continues through the cast-off edge.

163

Chapter 7
Knitting Patterns*
(3 patterns)

*Three fantastic patterns: two iconic designs and a new favourite. I love all three of them, each in their own way. They're like three best friends, each with their own talents. There's the sensible, classic one, the beautiful, exclusive one and the crazy, eccentric one. Try out different colour combinations and create exactly the sweater you've always dreamed of. But remember: the different designs have different shapes and silhouettes, so do check the chest measurement before you start.

"A dependable classic, a very popular sweater and a pullover that looks harder than it is."

Pattern
The No Limits Sweater

You can knit this in a single colour or use one of the three Scrap techniques.

One colour	Knit with 2 strands basic yarn.
ATS (p. 102)	Knit with 2 strands basic yarn and inserted scrap strands.
All Over (p. 106)	Knit with 1 strand of basic yarn and 1 scrap strand all over.
Bad Idea (p. 110)	Knit with 1, 2 3 or 4 scrap strands to achieve the right tension. You will need to knit a tension square (p. 44).
Basic yarn	e.g. Lima (50 g = approx. 100 m) (p. 263, Yarn qualities and Alternatives).
Scrap yarn	Shorter or longer strands for ATS. Knotted balls/skeins for All Over. Scrap yarn in all colours and shades for Bad Idea (p. 97, Scrap Yarn).
Size	1 (2) 3 (4) 5 (6) 7 (8) (p. 66, Sizes).
Bust measurement of the garment	Approx. 101 (110) 122 (131) 141 (149) 162 (170) cm. Overall chest measurement, measured directly under the armholes on the knitting (p. 66, Sizes).
Overall length	Approx. 51 (54) 57 (60) 64 (67) 70 (73) cm from shoulder to bottom edge.

Yarn requirements

One colour	14 (16) 17 (19) 20 (22) 24 (26) balls Lima.
ATS	Approx. 12 (14) 15 (17) 18 (20) 22 (24) balls Lima + at least 150 g scrap yarn.
All Over	Approx. 8 (8) 9 (10) 11 (13) 15 (17) balls Lima + at least 200 g scrap yarn.
Bad Idea	Approx. 600 (700) 750 (850) 900 (1000) 1100 (1200) g scrap yarn (p. 260, Yarn Requirements).
Needles	Circular needle size 9 (80 cm; for front, back + yoke), double-pointed needles size 9 (for sleeves, unless you knit with *Magic Loop*), circular needle size 6 (60 cm; for cuffs), double-pointed needles size 6 (for sleeve cuffs, unless you knit with *Magic Loop*), crochet hook size 6 (to crochet pieces together).
Tension square	Approx. 11 stitches and 17 rows stocking stitch with 2 strands of yarn on size 9 needles = 10 x 10 cm (p. 44, Tension Square). If your tension square is bigger, try thinner needles. If it's smaller, try thicker ones.

This sweater is an indestructible Lærke classic. I've knitted countless versions over the past ten years, and it's the first pullover I was ever truly satisfied to have knitted. It's extremely resilient.

It's knitted with two strands of yarn from bottom (p. 54) to top and can be varied in all sorts of ways. There's a beginner's version with straight cuffs and edgings (or 'welts') and a version for slightly more experienced knitters with turnaround rows à la Lærke Bagger. Check the chest size when choosing which size to knit. This design is fairly loose-fitting.

The version for more experienced knitters starts with rows where you continually increase stitches for the front (p. 62). This gives the pullover a rounded shape and makes the back look longer than the front. The bottom welt is the last part of the piece that you knit. It will be better if you do this before you finish the rest of the pullover. It's nicer and more motivating and it will give you a better feel for the length of the pullover. The beginner-friendly version is knitted on a circular needle throughout. You can also decide whether you prefer a long roll-neck collar or a neckband that's folded over and stitched or crocheted down on the inside (p. 56). Decreasing (p. 61) will give both versions of the pullover a cool pear shape – yes, you read that correctly. And apart from that, there are no limits for you.

>

166   Knitting Patterns

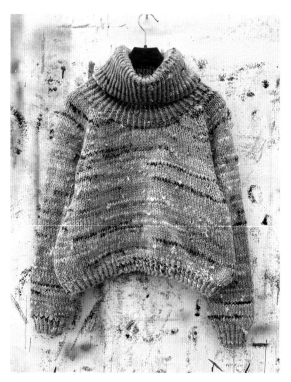

ATS (p. 102).

Bad Idea (p. 110).

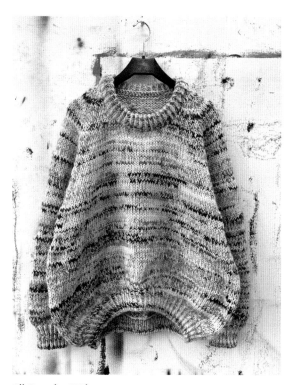

All Over (p. 106).

All Over (p. 106).

The No Limits
Sweater with a roll-
neck. Knitted in
olive-green basic yarn
in the All Over Scrap
technique (p. 106).

Basic pattern
The No Limits Sweater

All Over Scrap technique (p. 106). With pink basic yarn.

Beginners' version, front and back
Cast on 128 (136) 152 (160) 172 (180) 196 (204) stitches with circular needle size 6. Join up the stitches to make a circle and mark the beginning of the round, i.e. the 1st side of the pullover. Knit in twisted rib (k1 tbl, p1, repeat). 1st round: Rib 64 (68) 76 (80) 86 (90) 98 (102) stitches, set a marker for the other side of the pullover, then continue to end of round. Knit 5 (5) 6 (6) (7) 7 (8) 8 cm in twisted rib. Change to circular needle size 9 and knit in stocking stitch. When your work is 4 (4) 5 (5) 6 (6) 7 (7) cm from the top of the rib section, decrease 2 stitches on both sides as follows: * after the 1st marker k2, k2 tog (p. 61), knit until 4 stitches before the next marker, dec 1 (sl1 k1 psso) (p. 61), k2,*, repeat from * to the end of the round. Repeat this decrease round every 4 (4) 5 (5) 6 (6) 7 (7) cm, a total of 4 times = 112 (120) 136 (144) 156 (164) 180 (188) stitches. When your work is 29 (29) 31 (33) 35 (37) 40 (42) cm including the welt, cast off 2 (2) 3 (3) 4 (4) 5 (5) stitches for the armholes on both sides of the markers = 104 (112) 124 (132) 140 (148) 160 (168) stitches. Cut off the yarn and put your work to one side.

Version for more experienced knitters, front and back Cast on 64 (68) 76 (80) 86 (90) 98 102 stitches with circular needle size 9 for the back. Set a marker on both sides of these 64 (68) 76 (80) 86 (90) 98 102 stitches to indicate the sections of the sweater. Note: At first you'll knit in rows even though you've cast on with a circular needle. Knit one row plain knitting and continually cast on 5 (5) 6 (6) 7 (7) 8 (8) additional stitches on the other side of the marker (p. 62). On the return row, knit in purl and continually cast on 5 (5) 6 (6) 7 (7) 8 (8) additional stitches on the other side of the marker. Knit one row plain knitting and continually cast on 5 (5) 6 (6) 7 (7) 8 (8) additional stitches.

On the return row, knit in purl and continually cast on 5 (5) 6 (6) 7 (7) 8 (8) additional stitches. Repeat this 4 times more on each side, i.e. a total of 6 times on each side = 124 (128) 148 (152) 170 (174) 194 (198) stitches. Knit one row of plain knitting and continually cast on 2 (4) 2 (4) 1 (3) 1 (3) new stitches. On the return row, knit in purl and continually cast on 2 (4) 2 (4) 1 (3) 1 (3) new stitches = 128 (136) 152 (160) 172 (180) 196 (204) stitches. Now you've gradually cast on the stitches you need for the front of the sweater.

Next, knit 1 row in plain knitting across all the stitches. At the end of the row, join up the stitches to make a circle. From now on, knit in rounds. Continue in stocking stitch until you reach the 1st marker = beginning of the round. When your work measures 4 (4) 5 (5) 6 (6) 7 (7) cm at the centre front from the row when you joined the two ends together, start decreasing on both sides as follows: * after the 1st marker k2, k2 tog (p. 61) knit until 4 stitches before the next marker, dec 1 (sl1 k1 psso) (p. 61), k2,*, repeat from * to the end of the round. Repeat this decrease round every 4 (4) 5 (5) 6 (6) 7 (7) cm, a total of 4 times = 112 (120) 136 (144) 156 (164) 180 (188) stitches. When your work measures 20 (22) 24 (26) 28 (30) 32 (34) cm at the centre front from the row when you joined the two ends together, cast off 2 (2) 3 (3) 4 (4) 5 (5) stitches for the armholes on both sides of the markers = 104 (112) 124 (132) 140 (148) 160 (168) stitches. Cut off the yarn and put your work to one side.

Sleeves (both versions) Cast on 30 (32) 34 (36) 38 (40) 42 (44) stitches on double-pointed needles size 6 (or circular needle and Magic Loop, p. 41). Join up the stitches to make a circle and knit 6 cm in twisted rib (k1 tbl, p1, repeat). Change to double-pointed needles size 9 (or circular needle and Magic Loop) and knit in stocking

stitch in rounds. Mark the beginning of the round. Continue in stocking stitch, and in the 5th round above the cuff increase 1 stitch on each side of the marker (p. 61) as follows: k2, inc 1, continue in stocking stitch to the last 2 stitches, inc 1, k2. Increase as described in every 5th round a total of 9 times = 48 (50) 52 (54) 56 (58) 60 (62) stitches. Continue until your work measures 44 (44) 46 (46) 46 (46) 48 (48) cm or is as long as you want it. (Measure from wrist to armhole. If necessary, try on the sleeve). Cast off 2 (2) 3 (3) 4 (4) 5 (5) for the armholes on both sides of the markers = 44 (46) 46 (48) 48 (50) 50 (52) stitches. Cut off the yarn, put to one side and knit the 2nd sleeve in the same way.

Yoke (both versions) Place all sections on circular needle size 9, setting the sleeves above the armholes on the back and front. Place a marker between the right sleeve and the back – i.e. the sleeve to your right when you lay the knitting flat on the table with the back uppermost = the start of each round. Insert a marker and knit 1 round in stocking stitch, setting a marker for each transition between the different pieces for the yoke = a total of 4 markers, including the marker at beginning of the round. In the next row, decrease for the raglan. To do this, * k1, k2 tog (p. 61), continue in stocking stitch until 3 stitches before the marker, dec 1 (sl1 k1 psso) (p. 61), k1. Slip the marker from the left-hand needle to the right-hand needle, repeat from * to end. Repeat this on every 2nd row. Continue decreasing for the raglan until 38 (38) 40 (40) 42 (42) 44 (44) stitches remain on the yoke front. The next round you knit should be a row without decreases. Next round: On the front, cast off the middle 10 (10) 12 (12) 14 (14) 16 (16) stitches for the neck opening, knit to end of round. Cut off the yarn. Slide all the stitches from one needle to the other

without knitting them. Now start the neck opening on the left side of the knitting and the right sight of your work – i.e. the side on your left when you lay the knitting flat on the table with the front uppermost. Now knit stocking stitch in rows.

Cast off for the neck opening while continuing to decrease for the raglan on the right side of your work. For the neck opening, cast off 2 stitches at beginning of row, knit to end. In the next row, cast off 2 stitches at beginning of row and then purl to the end. Remember the BUTT for the edges, as it will be easier to pick up the stitches for the neckband later on. In the next 4 rows, cast off one stitch at beginning of each row. Continue in stocking stitch in rows, with the raglan decreases as before on the right side of your work, until 2 stitches remain before the markers on the front pieces. Cast off all remaining stitches with the right side of your work facing you.

Version for more experienced knitters: welt at bottom of sweater Start from the beginning of the round on the right side of the work. Using circular needle size 6, pick up 9 stitches for every 10 stitches – i.e. miss out every tenth stitch all the way round the bottom of the sweater. Then knit a total of 5 (5) 6 (6) (7) 7 (8) 8 cm in twisted rib (k1 tbl, p1). Cast off, keeping to the pattern: k1 over k1 tbl, p1 over p1 tbl.

Finishing and roll-neck Sew or crochet the armholes together inside the work, (p. 58). Darn in or knot all yarn ends (p. 100). If you're doing a roll-neck, knit in double twisted rib (k1 tbk, p1 tbl) (p. 29) so that both sides of the roll-neck collar look equally good. Starting to work in the middle of the back, with the right side of the work facing you (p. 56), use a circular needle size 6, to pick up 9 stitches for every 10 stitches around the neck opening. Make sure you end up with an even number of stitches. Then knit 30 cm or the

desired length in double twisted rib (k1 tbl, p1 tbl) in rounds. (Remember the roll-neck will be folded double.) Cast off loosely, keeping to the pattern. It's difficult to cast off loosely, but it's important (k1 over k1 tbl, p1 over p1 tbl). Fold the roll-neck collar over to the outside.

Finishing and folded-in neckband Sew or crochet the armholes together inside the work, (p. 58). Darn in or knot all yarn ends (p. 100). Working from the middle of the back, with the right side of the work facing you (p. 56), use a circular needle size 6 to pick up 9 stitches for every 10 stitches around the neck opening. Make sure you end up with an even number of stitches. Then knit 7 cm in twisted rib (k1 tbl, p1). Cast off loosely in plain knitting. Fold the neckband towards the inside of the pullover and crochet it down in slip stitch (p. 49) – or loosely stitch it into place.

171

Pattern
The Ombré T-shirt

You can only knit the Ombré T-Shirt using the All Over technique.

Basic yarn in plum and purple. For this version I only used scrap yarn in blue, black, brown and white.

All Over (p. 102)	Knit with 3 strands of basic yarn and 1 scrap yarn All Over. You will need to knit a tension square (p. 44).
Basic yarn	e.g. Silk Kid Mohair (25 g = ca. 210 m) (p. 263, Yarn Types and Alternatives).
Scrap yarn	Knotted balls/skeins for All Over. (p. 97, Scrap yarn).
Size	1 (2) 3 (4) 5 (6) 7 (8) (p. 66, sizes).
Chest measurement of the garment	Approx. 92 (100) 108 (116) 124 (132) 140 (148) cm. Overall chest measurement, measured directly under the armholes on the knitting (p. 66, Sizes).
Overall length	Approx. 47 (50) 53 (57) 60 (63) 66 (67) cm from shoulder to bottom edge.

Yarn requirements

With folded-over neckband	Approx. 4 (5) 6 (7) 7 (8) 9 (10) balls Silk Kid Mohair (Basic yarn B). Approx. 1 (2) 2 (3) 3 (4) 5 (6) balls Silk Kid Mohair as accent (Basic yarn A) + at least 150 g scrap yarn.
With roll-neck collar	+ 1 balls Silk Kid Mohair (Basic yarn B) + at least 50 g scrap yarn extra (p. 260, Estimated yarn requirement).
Needles	Circular needle size 10 (80 cm; for front, back + yoke), double-pointed needles size 10 (for the sleeves, unless you knit with *Magic Loop*), 2 circular needles size 10 6 (60 cm) (for the edging), double-pointed needles size 6 (for the sleeve edging, unless you knit with *Magic Loop*), circular needle size 5 (60 cm) (for the turned-back band of purl knitting on the bottom edge), crochet hook size 6 (to crochet pieces together).
Tension square	Approx. 10 stitches and 14 rows stocking stitch with 3 strands of mohair and 1 scrap strand on size 10 needles = 10 x 10 cm (p. 44, tension square). If your tension square is bigger, try thinner needles. If it's smaller, try thicker ones.

This T-shirt is truly cool, so don't be sad that it can only be knitted with one technique. It's an *all-time favourite* that lots of people have asked for. It's a perfectly ordinary raglan shirt but doesn't look in the least bit ordinary. I remember I had no idea what I was even making here until it was finished. Boy, was I proud of it! It was simply a winner – what more can I say? It's quick to knit, truly fantastic, and you can design it whatever way you like.

It's knitted with four strands – 3 strands of Silk Kid Mohair and 1 strand of scrap yarn – from bottom to top. The hems are knitted in stocking stitch and folded in instead of being ribbed welts. You use two different colours of basic yarn (Silk Kid Mohair) to create the colour gradient known as "ombre". The ombré effect happens when you gradually replace the strands of the first basic colour, one by one, with those of your second basic yarn colour. By the end you will be knitting in a completely different colour from the one you started with. Only the bottom part of the T-shirt is knitted with the ombre effect.

When you change colours, you can darn the ends in. But I prefer to cut the thread off and knot it with the next yarn (p. 100) as close as possible to the beginning of the round. You won't see the joins anyway. Knit the scrap strand as an auxiliary strand all the way through. Decide for yourself whether you prefer a long, 1990s roll-neck collar or a folded-in neckband. Depending on how dramatic you want your T-shirt to be, choose a basic yarn in colours that blend or contrast with each other. You can also choose a really playful range of colours for your scrap threads compared with your basic yarn if you like. But if you prefer a calmer design, choose colour shades that are similar to each other (p. 174).

>

Basic in white and red.

Basic in white and curry.

Basic in black and pink.

Basic in dark blue and light blue.

Basic in white
and yellow.

Basic pattern
The Ombré T-shirt

Colours

Basic yarn A (accent colour for the bottom)

Basic yarn B (main colour for the rest)

Front and back Cast on 92 (100) 108 (116) 124 (132) 140 (148) stitches with circular needle size 6 using 3 strands of basic yarn A and 1 scrap strand. Join up the stitches to make a circle and mark the beginning of the round = one side of the T-shirt. Knit in stocking stitch in rounds. In the 1st round knit 46 (50) 54 (58) 62 (66) 70 (74) stitches and set a marker for the other side of the T-shirt. Continue knitting for a total of 9 (9) 9 (9) 11 (11) 11 (11) rounds. Change to circular needle size 5 and knit 1 round in purl, as this will mark more clearly and durably the edge where the bottom hem will be folded back. Change back to circular needle size 6 and continue in stocking stitch for a total of 10 (10) 10 (10) 12 (12) 12 (12) further rounds. Now complete the bottom hem. To do this, use another size 6 circular needle to pick up 92 (100) 108 (116) 124 (132) 140 (148) stitches at the bottom from the cast-on edge. Important: make sure you pick up the right number of stitches. Otherwise you'll end up with wonky edges. Not good! Now, fold the hem upwards so that the picked-up stitches are on the inside of your work. This will more or less form a tunnel with the wrong sides facing each other on the inside. You now have two circular needles, both with stitches on them, lying parallel beside each other. Knit into the stitch on the front needle and the stitch on the back needle at the same time, with a knit stitch. Do this with each stitch until you've knitted all the stitches from both needles together. Now you've finished the hem. Change to circular needle size 10 and knit 4 rounds.

Replace 1 strand of basic yarn A with 1 strand of basic yarn B (= 2 strands A, 1 strand B, 1 strand scrap) and knit 4 rounds. Do the same

again: replace 1 strand of basic yarn A with 1 strand of basic yarn B (= 1 strand A, 2 strands B, 1 strand scrap) and knit 4 rounds. And again: replace the final strand of basic yarn A with 1 strand of basic yarn B (= 3 strands B, 1 strand scrap) and continue with plain knitting in stocking stitch until your work measures 30 (32) 34 (36) 38 (40) 42 (44) cm or the required length. Cast off 3 (3) 4 (4) 4 (5) 5 (5) stitches for the armholes on both sides of the markers = 80 (88) 92 (100) 108 (112) 120 (128) stitches. Cut off the yarn and put your work to one side.

Sleeves (both the same) Cast on 36 (40) 44 (48) 52 (56) 60 (64) stitches with circular needle size 6 using 3 strands of basic yarn B and 1 scrap strand. Mark the beginning of the round. Knit a total of 5 (5) 5 (5) 6 (6) 6 (6) rounds in plain knitting (stocking stitch). As on the front and back section, change to circular needle size 5 and knit 1 round in purl, then change back to circular needle size 6 and knit another 6 (6) 6 (6) 7 (7) 7 (7) rounds in plain knitting. Work the hem for the sleeves in exactly the same way as for the front and back section. In other words, pick up 36 (40) 44 (48) 52 (56) 60 (64) stitches at the bottom from the cast-on edge using another size 6 circular needle. Fold the hem upwards inside your work, and in plain knitting, knit into the stitch on the front needle and the stitch on the back needle at the same time. Change to circular needle size 10 and knit 9 (9) 10 (10) 11 (11) 12 (12) rounds. In the next row cast off 3 (3) 4 (4) 4 (5) 5 (5) stitches for the armholes on both sides of the markers = 30 (34) 36 (40) 44 (46) 50 (54) Cut off the yarn and put your work to one side. Knit the 2nd sleeve in the same way.

Yoke Transfer all the sections you've knitted onto a circular needle size 10, setting the sleeves above the armholes on the back and front. Place a marker between the right sleeve

and the back – i.e. the sleeve to your right when you lay the knitting out flat in front of you with the back uppermost = the start of each round. Re-join the yarn here (3 strands of basic yarn B and 1 scrap strand) and knit 1 round in plain knitting, setting a marker for each transition between the different pieces for the yoke = a total of 4 markers, including the one at beginning of the round.

In the next row decrease for the raglan: * k1, k2 tog (p. 61), continue in plain knitting until 3 stitches before the marker, dec 1 (sl1 k1 psso) (p. 61), k1*. Slip the marker from the left-hand needle to the right-hand needle, repeat from * to the end of the round. Repeat the raglan decrease on every 2nd row after that until 30 (32) 36 (40) 42 (46) 46 (50) stitches remain on the yoke front. The next round you knit should be a row without decreases. In that round, cast off the middle 6 (6) 8 (8) 8 (10) 10 (10) stitches for the neck opening, then knit to end of round. Cut off the yarn.

Slide all the stitches from one needle to the other without knitting them. Now you can begin the neck opening on the left-hand side of the knitting – that is, the side on your left when you lay the knitting with the front uppermost flat on the table – with the right side of your work facing you. Now continue in stocking stitch, in rows rather than rounds.

Cast off for the neck opening while continuing to decrease for the raglan. To do this, cast off 2 stitches at beginning of next two rows for the neck opening as follows: cast off 2 stitches at beginning of row, knit to end of the row, then in the next row, cast off 2 stitches at beginning of row and then purl to the end of the row. Don't forget the BUTT for the edge stitches as it will make it easier to pick up the stitches for the neckband later on. In the next 4 rows, cast off one stitch at beginning of each row. Continue to knit stocking stitch in rows, with the raglan decreases as before on the right

side of your work until 2 stitches remain before the markers on the front pieces. Cast off all remaining stitches on the right side.

Finishing and roll-neck Sew or crochet the armholes together in the inside of the work (p. 58). Darn in or knot all yarn ends (p. 100). If you decide on a roll-neck, knit in double twisted rib (k1 tbl, p1 tbl) (p. 29). That way roll-neck will look good inside and out. Start to work in the middle of the back, with the right side of your work facing you (p. 56). Using circular needle size 6, and 3 strands of basic yarn B plus 1 scrap strand, pick up 9 stitches for every 10 stitches around the neck opening, making sure you end up with an even num-ber of stitches. Then knit approx. 30 cm or the desired length. Cast off loosely, keeping to the pattern (k1 over k1 tbl, p1 over p1 tbl). It's difficult to cast off loosely, but it's important. Fold the roll-neck collar over to the outside.

Finishing and crew neck folded in and stitched/crocheted in place Sew or crochet the armholes together in the inside of the work (p. 58). Darn in or knot all yarn ends (p. 100). Start to work in the middle of the back, with the right side of your work facing you (p. 56). Using circular needle size 6, and 3 strands of basic yarn B plus 1 scrap strand, pick up 9 stitches for every 10 stitches around the neck opening, making sure you end up with an even number of stitches. Then knit 7 cm in twisted rib (k1 tbl, p1). Cast off loosely using plain knitting. Fold the neckband in towards the inside of the pullover and crochet the edge down around the neck opening using slip stitch (p. 49), or loosely stitch into place. For a folded-down neckband like this, there's no need to twist the purl stitches because only one side of the neckband is visible. You only need to twist the purl stitches (p1 tbl) when both sides of the collar are visible (e.g. polo or roll-necks). Knitting into the backs of purl stitches really sucks, so it's best avoided!

The Not So Heavy Sweater

You can knit this in a single colour or use one of the three Scrap techniques.

One colour	Knit with 2 strands of basic yarn (e.g. Naturuld and Superwash Vital).
ATS (p. 102)	Knit with 2 strands of basic yarn (e.g. Naturuld and Superwash Vital) and inserted scrap strands.
All Over (p. 106)	Knit with 1 strand of basic yarn (1 B) and 1 scrap strand all over.
Bad Idea (p. 110)	Knit with 1, 2 3 or 4 scrap strands to achieve the right tension. You will need to knit a tension square (p. 44).
Basic yarn	e.g. Naturuld (100 g = 100 m), Superwash Vital (50 g = 115 m) (p. 263, Yarn Types and Alternatives).
Scrap yarn	Shorter or longer strands for ATS. Knotted balls/skeins for All Over. Scrap yarn in all colours and shades for Bad Idea (p. 97, Scrap Yarn).
Size	1 (2) 3 (4) 5 (6) 7 (8) (p. 66, Sizes).
Chest measurement of the garment	Approx. 96 (104) 112 (124) 132 (140) 152 (160) cm + approx. 2 cm for the seams on the outside (1 cm extra per side seam). Overall chest measurement, measured directly under the armholes on the knitting (p. 66, Sizes).
Overall length	Approx. 49 (51) 54 (56) 59 (61) 63 (65) from the shoulder to the bottom edge.

Yarn requirements

One colour	Approx. 8 (8) 10 (11) 11 (12) 13 (14) balls Naturuld + 8 (9) 10 (11) 12 (13) 13 (14) balls Superwash Vital.
ATS	Approx. 8 (8) 10 (11) 11 (12) 13 (14) balls Naturuld + 5 (6) 7 (8) 9 (10) 11 (12) balls Superwash Vital + at least 100 g scrap yarn.
All Over	Approx. 8 (8) 10 (11) 11 (12) 13 (14) balls Naturuld + at least 250 g scrap.
Bad Idea	Approx. 800 (850) 900 (950) 1000 (1050) 1100 (1200) g scrap yarn (p. 260, Yarn Requirements).
Needles	Circular needle size 10 (80 cm; for sleeves and front and back sections + upper section of the yoke), circular needle size 9 (80 or 100 cm; for the 1st part of the yoke), circular needle size 6 (60 or 80 cm; for cuffs), crochet hook size 6 (to crochet pieces together).

Tension square   10 stitches and 20 rows garter stitch on size 10 needles = 10 x 10 cm (p. 44, tension square). If your tension square is bigger, try thinner needles. If it's smaller, try thicker ones.

I really like knitting in garter stitch. It looks so *old school* and takes me right back to my youth, when I was still an inexperienced knitter. Knitting in garter stitch makes me feel like a fantastic world has just opened up for me, as if everything has just begun. This pullover is fantastic in a very cool way. It looks really hard to make, but it isn't.

The pullover is knitted in rows with two strands of yarn. The front, back and sleeves are knitted in garter stitch from bottom to top. For the yoke, you put the pieces together on the circular needle and then alternate between 1 round of plain knitting and 1 round of purl. You do the raglan decreases in the plain rounds. When you divide the work for the neck opening, you go back to plain knitting in every row. Then you join up the side and sleeve seams. The yoke is knitted in rounds on a finer needle to achieve the same tension as when you are knitting in rows. The right side of the knitting – the side that will be on the outside – where the cast-on thread is on the right when you lay the work in front of you on the table. You need to know which side is which when you are assembling all the pieces for the yoke, because otherwise the loops of the garter stitch won't match up when you crochet the pieces together.

>

ATS (p. 102).

ATS (p. 102).

All Over (p. 106).

All Over (p. 106).

The Not So Heavy
Sweater knitted with
a basic yarn in navy
blue and in the
All Over Scrap
technique (p. 106).

Basic pattern
The Not So Heavy Sweater

A cup of coffee, basic yarn in beige and All Over Scrap technique (p. 106).

Back Cast on 52 (56) 60 (66) 70 (74) 80 (84) stitches with circular needle size 6 and knit in plain knitting (garter stitch) in rows. Don't forget the BUTT for the edge stitch (p. 37). After 12 (12) 12 (12) 14 (14) 14 (14) rows, change to needle size 10. Knit until your work reaches an overall length of 20 (22) 24 (26) 28 (30) 32 (34) cm. Then, on the right side of your work, dec 1 stitch on both ends of the row as follows: BUTT stitch at the edge, k1 (sl1 k1 psso) (p. 61), knit to 4 stitches before the end of the row, k2tog (p. 61), k2. Continue in plain knitting until your work measures 26 (28) 30 (32) 34 (36) 38 (40) cm, then dec 1 stitch at both ends of the row as described above. Continue to knit in plain knitting until your work measures 28 (30) 32 (34) 36 (38) 40 (42) cm. Make sure the cast-on yarn end is hanging down at bottom right, then the right side will be uppermost facing you. In the next 2 rows cast off 3 (3) 3 (4) 4 (4) 5 (5) stitches for the armholes at beginning of row = 42 (46) 50 (54) 58 (62) 66 (70) stitches. Cut off the yarn and put the work to one side.

Front Work as for the back, making sure you knit exactly the same number of rows. That will be important later on when you finish the pullover.

Sleeves (both the same) Cast on 25 (28) 31 (34) 37 (40) 43 (46) stitches with circular needle size 6 and knit in plain knitting (garter stitch). Don't forget the BUTT for the edge stitch (p. 37). After 16 rows, on a right-side row, inc 1 stitch in every 3rd stitch (including the edge stitch) (p. 61), ending with k1 as your edge stitch at the end of the row = 33 (37) 41 (45) 49 (53) 57 (61) stitches. Change to needle size 10 and continue knitting without further increases until your work measures 42 (42) 44 (44) 44 (46) 46 (46) cm or the required length, measured from wrist to armhole. Make sure the cast-on yarn end is hanging down at bottom right, then the right side will be uppermost facing you. In the next 2 rows cast off 3 (3) 3 (4) 4 (4) 5 (5) stitches for the armholes at beginning of row. Cut off the yarn and put the work to one side = 27 (31) 35 (37) 41 (45) 47 (51). Knit the 2nd sleeve in the same way.

Yoke Change to circular needle size 9 to achieve the right tension. Now knit 1 round in plain knitting and 1 round in purl alternately. Important: Make sure the outside of the pieces is facing you when you put them on your circular needle. Check this by ensuring the cast-on yarn end hangs down on the right-hand side of the work. Arrange all the pieces on circular needle size 9, setting the sleeves above the armholes on the back and fronts: first the back, then the left sleeve, then the front, then the right sleeve. Set a marker between the right sleeve and the back – i.e. the sleeve on your right when the knitting is lying on the table with the back facing uppermost = beginning of the round. Join the yarn here and, with two strands, knit 1 round in plain knitting, setting a marker for each transition between the different pieces for the yoke = 4 markers incl. the beginning of the round. In the next round, purl all the way round. In the next round – a plain knitting round again – decrease for the raglan as follows: * k1, k2 tog (p. 61), continue in plain knitting until 3 stitches before the next marker, dec 1 (sl1 k1 psso) (p. 61), k1*. Slip the marker from the left-hand needle to the right-hand needle, repeat from * to end and repeat on every plain knitting row. Knit alternately 1 round purl and 1 round plain knit-ting while continuing to decrease for the raglan until 30 (34) 36 (40) 42 (46) 46 (50) stitches remain on the front. The next round should be a purl round. Here, cast off purlwise the middle 6 (8) 8 (8) 8 (10) 10 (10) stitches for the front of the neck opening, then continue to end of round. Cut off the yarn. Slide all the stitches from one needle to the other without knitting them. Now you can begin the neck opening on the left side of the knitting – i.e. the side on your left when you lay the knitting flat on the table with the front uppermost – and the right side of your work facing you.

Now knit in plain knitting (garter stitch) in rows again. Change to needle size 10 and continue to knit the decreases for the raglan. At the same time, cast off 2 stitches at beginning of next 2 rows as follows: cast off 2 stitches at beginning of row, knit to end of the row; in the next row, cast off 2 stitches at beginning of row, knit in plain knitting to the end of the row. Don't forget the BUTT for the edge stitches: It'll make it easier to pick up the stitches for the neckband later on. In the next 4 rows, cast off in the same way at beginning of row. Continue to knit in garter stitch, decreasing for the raglan with the right side of the work facing you, until 2 stitches remain before the markers on the front pieces. Cast off all remaining stitches on the right side.

Finishing and neckband Crochet the side seams and sleeve seams together using slip stitch (p. 49) and 1 strand Naturuld. With the right side of your work facing you, insert the crochet hook through the 1st loop of the edge stitch. (Inserting it through both loops will make the seam too thick.) If you're a fan of symmetry, start one side seam at the bottom edge and the other at

182 Knitting Patterns

the top edge, from the armhole, in other words. Then the seams will look the same. Try it out. It's not essential, but it's a nice detail. Close the sleeve seams on the inside (p. 58). Darn in or knot the ends of the yarn (p. 100).

Neckband Starting to work in the middle of the back, with the right side of the work facing you (p. 56), use a size 6 circular needle to pick up 9 stitches for every 10 stitches around the neck opening. Starting with a purl round, knit a total of 5 rounds, alternating between 1 round in purl and 1 round in plain. On the 6th round (plain knitting) cast off evenly and loosely. Darn in or knot the ends.

Chapter 8
Embroidery

"About (almost) embroidering the Meaning of Life, going totally stitch crazy and definitely fancying a pizza."

DUPLICATE STITCH (SWISS DARNING)

Want to put your own personal mark on your knitting? Of course you do! Tried duplicate stitch yet? It's probably the most fun way of putting your stamp on something. I love the fact that you can do it however you like. You decide how large or small your motif will be – whether a tiny heart or a great big yin-yang symbol. When you fancy a break from knitting, a little interim project can be worth its weight in gold, and compared with other techniques in the book, embroidering with duplicate stitch is much less full-on. Give it a try. You might decide it's the worst thing you ever did, never to do it again, and the undo the whole lot – by which time you'll only have wasted about three quarters of an hour. But you might equally well discover how awesome it is to "paint" on your knitting with a needle – and end up spending days or maybe even weeks on your new craze.

You do duplicate stitch with the right side of your stocking-stitch piece facing you. As the name suggests, this stitch duplicates the V shape of the knitted stitches. The finished result looks like knitting but isn't. Duplicate stitch is like painting on knitting and great fun to do. It's a really good way to personalise your knitting. You can embroider large motifs or small, freehand or following a diagram – a pixelated image of a motif (p. 196), in other words. It looks complicated, but isn't, I promise! Scrap yarn is the perfect thing to use.

A few years ago, when I was pregnant with my son, I suffered from nest-building syndrome and started tidying up and throwing out unwanted stuff like crazy. I checked through a lot of old stuff I had lying around and became completely obsessed by my old pencil case and exercise books from primary school, because they were a short, personal window onto my unfiltered thoughts at the time: "I love Marco", and Alexander, and Kasper, and definitely also Nicklas. And then there were the little doodles from when I was bored in physics lessons. I suddenly decided I wanted to make a modern version of those exercise books and the pencil case, translated into a sweater: a pullover, naive and direct, and at the same time a mirror of the present. I called it the *Meaning of Life* Sweater.

Duplicate stitch was the perfect technique, because I could work with very small motifs and just do bits whenever I felt like it. I never completely finished the sweater, not because it was too hard or took too long but because I kept on thinking up new things to embroider onto it. Now it's become a sort of sketch pullover for me and just keeps more and more beautiful all the time.

So, start off with motifs you find cool. You can combine them as the mood takes you, all at the same time or just a few. Position them at random – that's what I do – in the middle, at the side, top, bottom, anywhere. The great thing about duplicate stitch is that you don't have to know where the middle is. Just hold the knitting in front of the mirror and decide where you think your motif would look good. I think placing the motifs right in the middle of a pullover is greatly overrated.

    You can embroider on all the designs in this book, unless they are in garter stitch or rib.

All the motifs on The Bad Idea Top (p. 226) were placed at random. I can't really say why I put them where they are.

A knitted stitch is shaped like a V, and when you duplicate it, you work from bottom to top. Cut a thread between 25 and 70 cm long – depending on how much embroidery you are planning to do.

Duplicate stitch in four steps

1 Insert your needle from back to front through Point 1. Leave about 10 cm of thread hanging on the underside. You will need this later to darn or knot the end (pp. 65 and 101).

2 Then insert the needle from front to back through Point 2.

3 Then insert the needle from back to front through Point 3.

4 Insert the needle from front to back through Point 1. Now you have made your first duplicate stitch. Insert the needle from back to front through Point 1 of the next stitch and repeat the steps above.

You can do duplicate stitch horizontally, vertically, diagonally, from right to left or from left to right. Just do what you find easiest, what feels right to you. Whichever direction you choose, it's always best to start at Point 1, at the bottom tip of the stitch (of the V), in other words. Whether you insert your needle through Point 2 or 3 first doesn't matter, as long as you end up at Point 1 again. When I work from right to left, I insert my needle through Point 2 first, before Point 3. When I work from left to right, then I insert it through Point 3 first.

MARK THE CENTRE

- If you want to position your motif in the middle of your knitting – on the front of a pullover or sock, for example – then mark the middle while you're knitting by inserting a thread into the centre stitch and knotting it. Don't remove it until you've positioned your motif. You can use the same method to position the motif at the side as well.

189

The same two
flower motifs on
The Not-So-Basic
Kid's Sweater
(p. 152), but as
mirror images so
they look different.
I stitched the long
stalk because it
looks good.
<

It also looks truly
awesome if you
embroider on
scrap yarn, as here
for The Cute Top
(p. 208).
>

- If you think your work is starting to look dreadful, don't despair! It's exactly what I always think. Totally stressful. When you look at it from a distance, it doesn't look hideous at all. It always looks great! Just relax.

- **Use a good embroidery needle:** Don't use a needle with a sharp point. Use one with a rounded tip so you don't split the threads of your knitting. Split threads are really stupid.

- **Never pull the stitch too tight:** The embroidered thread should be the same tension as your knitting, as it lies on top of the stitch. So don't pull it too tight. But don't leave it too loose either, of course!

- **Find the right type of yarn:** Finding the right yarn so it looks good on your knitting takes a bit of patience. Most embroidery books say you should use the same thickness of yarn as you used for your knitting. That is correct to some extent, but I've also used a thinner yarn successfully. Just try it out. You'll soon be able to tell if it's getting too thick and lumpy. If it is, change to a slightly thinner yarn.

- **Use cardboard:** If you're embroidering on a knitted item with more than one layer – a pullover or socks knitted on a round needle, for example – put a piece of cardboard between the layers so you don't stitch the two sides together by mistake.

- **Knot the ends:** I never darn the ends of the thread in, unless there's an uneven number or they're too far apart to knot. Instead I knot them together carefully on the wrong side of the knitting, taking care not to pull them too tight, and then I cut off the ends. I choose threads that are close together so they don't fly around all over the place on the inside of my knitting.

- **Embroider the outline first:** This is the black frame or edge of your motif. If you embroider it first, you can then fill it with colours. I find I make fewer mistakes that way.

- **Combination of motifs:** First of all, draw the entire motif – the words "I love pizza", or whatever – on a sheet of squared paper. Then you can play around with the position of your motifs so you don't regret anything later. You may need to count how many stitches wide and high your motif will be so you can find the right place for it. When you know what you're doing, start to embroider. You can also add circles, larger patches of colour or other things around your motifs. Stuff like that is really great fun.

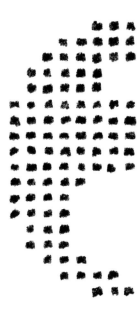

Duplicate stitch is just ultra-cool. The Nice Slipover (p. 202).

OMG, right?! Here I followed the tip on page p. 189 about marking the centre of the front with a thread so that I can place the motif exactly in the middle of the absolutely fantastic Carpe Diem Sweater (p. 252).

PATTERN DIAGRAMS

Now you are more than ready to start embroidering. You're welcome to use my motifs and just get going. In the diagram, each stitch is represented by a square. Count the squares and embroider wherever you like in whatever colours you choose.

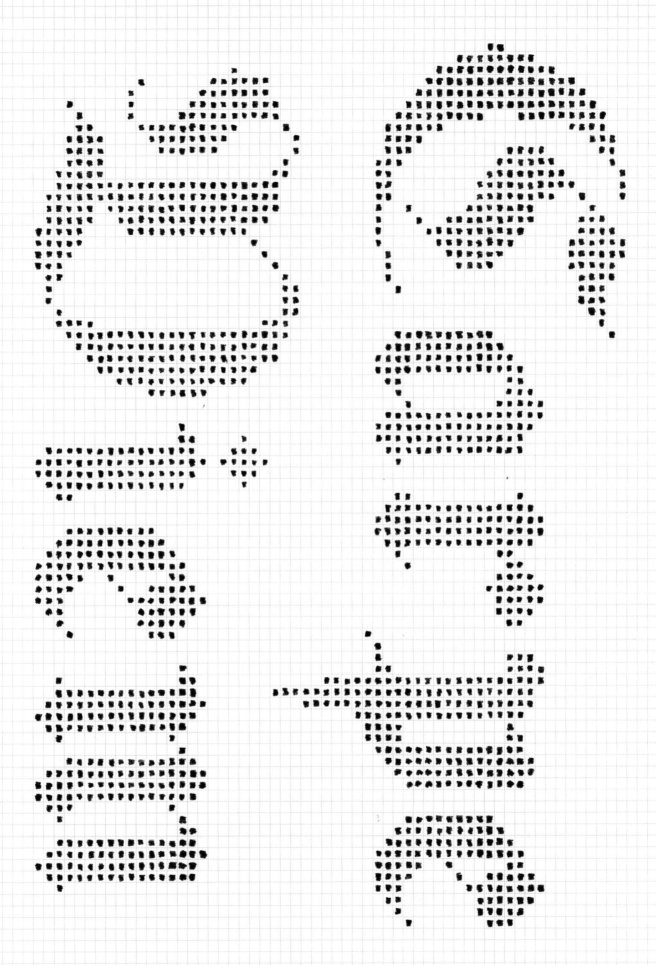

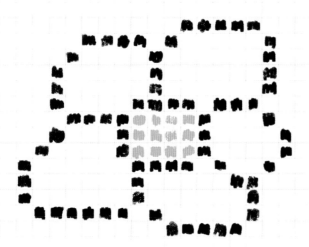

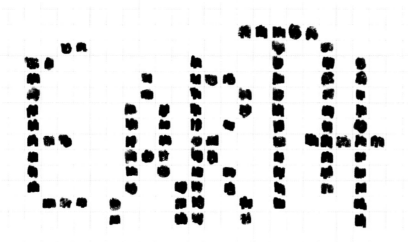

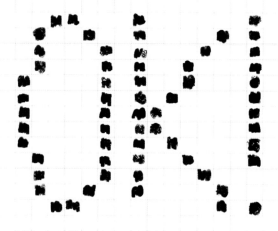

Chapter 9
Knitting Patterns*
(3 patterns)

*These three little patterns are quick to knit, so why not take a bit longer for the embroidery? If you've never knitted socks before, now is definitely the time to try. It's fun! But it's also a challenge, a bit like playing a computer game. There are a few hurdles involved and you have to work your way through some irritating and rather lengthy sequences on your way to the finish line. But when you get there, you will be showered with praise. First of all, though, here come the Nice Slipover and the Cute Top.

"The Nice Slipover, Cute Top (the cutest of its kind in the world!) and socks will teach you almost everything you need to know about knitting."

The Nice Slipover

You can knit this in a single colour or use one of the three Scrap techniques.

One colour	Knit with 2 strands basic yarn.
ATS (p. 102)	Knit with 2 strands basic yarn and inserted scrap strands.
All Over (p. 106)	Knit with 1 strand basic yarn and 1 scrap strand all over.
Bad Idea (p. 110)	Knit with 1, 2, 3 or 4 strands to get the right tension. You'll need to knit a tension square (p. 44).
Basic yarn	e.g. Lima (50 g = 100 m) (p. 263, Yarn Types and Alternatives).
Scrap yarn	Shorter or longer strands for ATS. Knotted balls/skeins for All Over. Scrap yarn in all colours and shades for Bad Idea (p. 97, Scrap yarn).
Size	1 (2) 3 (4) 5 (6) 7 (8) (p. 66, Sizes).
Chest measurement of the garment	Approx. 101 (110) 122 (131) 141 (149) 162 (170) cm. Overall chest measurement, measured directly under the armholes on the knitting (p. 66, Sizes).
Overall length	Approx. 48 (51) 54 (57) 60 (63) 66 (69) cm from shoulder to bottom edge.

Yarn requirements

With a flat neckband

One colour	Approx. 9 (10) 11 (12) 13 (15) 17 (18) balls Lima (p. 260, Yarn Requirements).
ATS	Approx. 8 (9) 10 (11) 12 (14) 16 (18) balls Lima + at least 50 g scrap yarn.
All Over	Approx. 5 (6) 7 (8) 9 (11) 12 (13) balls Lima + at least 150 g scrap yarn.
Bad Idea	Approx. 400 (450) 500 (550) 600 (650) 700 (750) g scrap yarn.
With a roll-neck collar	+ 2 balls Lima or 100 g scrap yarn.
Needles	Circular needle size 9 (80 cm; for front and back), circular needle size 6 (60 cm; for the neckband), crochet hook size 7 (to crochet together).
Tension square	11 stitches and 17 rows in stocking stitch on size 9 needles = 10 x 10 cm (p. 44, Tension square). If your tension square is bigger, try thinner needles. If it's smaller, try thicker ones.

This slipover is simply awesome! It has a few cute details and is really easy and quick to knit. Experiment with it and develop the design further: knit in your choice of colours and perhaps embroider it here and there with duplicate stitch.

The back and front of the sleeveless pullover are knitted together in rounds. Then you divide your work for the armholes before finishing the front and back sections separately. The shoulder seams are crocheted together.

If you're knitting in ATS or All Over, knit with two strands. For Bad Idea, knit with one, two, three or four strands. By the way, the neckband is almost the only one in this book that's not folded down, as it would be too thick and lumpy otherwise. You can make the slipover with a flat neckband or a polo neck like The No Limits Sweater (p. 166).

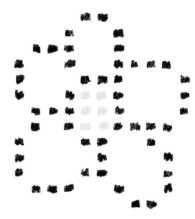

The Nice Slipover with embroidery (p. 186). The position of the motif is entirely random.

Single colour with embroidery (p. 186).

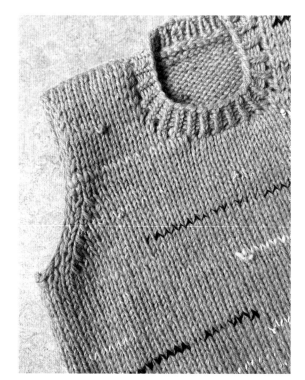

ATS (p. 102).

Bad Idea (p. 110).

All Over Scrap technique (p. 106), knitted with blue basic yarn and all the colours of the rainbow.

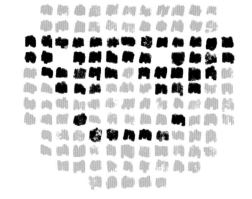

Basic pattern
The Nice Slipover

Front and back

Cast on 112 (120) 136 (144) 156 (164) 180 (188) stitches on circular needle size 6 with two strands. Join up the stitches to make a circle and mark the beginning of the round and one side of the slipover. Knit in twisted rib (k1 tbl, p1, repeat). 1st round: Knit 56 (60) 68 (72) 78 (82) 90 (94) stitches, set a marker = other side of the slipover. Continue to the end of the round in the same way. Knit 5 (5) 6 (6) (7) 7 (8) 8 cm in twisted rib, change to circular needle size 9 and continue in stocking stitch. When your work measures 29 (29) 31 (33) 35 (37) 40 (42) cm including the ribbing, cast off 2 (2) 3 (3) 4 (4) 5 (5) stitches for the armholes on both sides of the markers = 104 (112) 124 (132) 140 (148) 160 (168) stitches. Cut the yarn. You will knit the next sections of the front and back separately in rows on the circular needle.

Back

Start with the back section and with the right side facing towards you. Knit in rows in stocking stitch. On the 1st row (plain knitting) decrease for the raglan as follows: BUTT as edge stitch (p. 37), sl1 k1 psso (p. 61), knit to 4 stitches before the end of the row, k2 tog (p. 61), k2. Return row: BUTT as edge stitch, purl to last stitch, k1. Keeping the edge stitches as described, knit a total of 6 (6) 7 (7) 8 (8) 9 (9) rows with a raglan decrease, ending with a purl row = a total of 12 (12) 14 (14) 16 (16) 18 (18) rows after dividing the work into front and back sections. Continue knitting in stocking stitch without further decreases until the arm-

hole measures 21 (23) 25 (27) 29 (31) 33 (35) cm from the division. On the next row of plain knitting, cast off all stitches.

Front

Knit the front to match the back until you've completed all the decreases for the raglan. Next row (return row): BUTT as edge stitch, purl to last stitch, k1. Next row (plain knitting): Cast off the middle 8 (8) 10 (10) 12 (12) 14 (14) stitches for the neck opening and complete each side separately. Start with the left side – that is the side on your left when the slipover is lying flat on front of you, right side uppermost.

At beginning of next knit row, cast off two stitches. Next row (return row): BUTT as edge stitch, purl to last stitch, k1. Cast off 1 stitch at the neck edge at beginning of next two rows of plain knitting. Continue in stocking stitch without further decreases until the left front is as long as the back, i.e. 21 (23) 25 (27) 29 (31) 33 (35) cm. Cast off all stitches.

Knit the right front to match the left front, i.e. start with the inside of the slipover facing you and cast off two stitches for the neck opening. Next row: knit to end, then at beginning of next two purl rows, cast off 1 stitch at the neck edge. Continue in stocking stitch without further decreases until the left front is as long as the back. Cast off all stitches on the next row of plain knitting.

Neckband and completion

Turn the slipover inside out and crochet the shoulder seams together with slip stitch (p. 49). So

that the seams look the same on both sides, start one at the outer edge (the shoulder edge) and work the other from the neck opening outwards.

Neckband: Starting in the middle of the back, with the right side of the work facing you (p. 56), use a size 6 circular needle to pick up 9 stitches for every 10 stitches around the neck opening. Make sure you end up with an even number of stitches. Then knit 5 rounds in twisted rib (k1 tbl, p1). On the 6th round, cast off in rib (k stitches over k, p stitches over p). Starting at the bottom of the armhole (in the middle), insert your crochet hook into the next loop of the BUTT and crochet loosely round the armholes in slip stitch (p. 58). Darn in or knot the yarn ends (p. 100).

ATS Scrap technique (p. 102), knitted with a basic yarn in beige and just a few scrap threads.

Pattern
The Cute Top

You can knit this in a single colour or use one of the three Scrap techniques.

One colour	Knit with 1 strand basic yarn.
ATS (p. 102)	Knit with 1 strand basic yarn and inserted scrap strands.
All Over (p. 106)	Knit stripes with the basic yarn only, followed by stripes using the scrap yarn. All cuffs and rib sections are knitted in basic yarn.
Bad Idea (p. 110)	Knit with 1, 2 or 3 scrap strands to get the right tension. You will need to knit a tension square (p. 44).
Basic yarn	e.g. Merino Cotton or Superwash Vital (50 g = 120 m/115 m) (p. 263, Yarn Types and Alternatives).
Scrap yarn	Shorter or longer strands for ATS. Knotted balls/skeins for All Over. Scrap yarn in all colours and shades for Bad Idea (p. 97, Scrap Yarn).
Size	1 (2) 3 (4) 5 (6) 7 (8) (p. 66, Sizes).
Chest measurement of the garment	Approx. 75 (82) 89 (96) 104 (111) 118 (125) cm. Overall measurement, measured directly under the armholes on the top (p. 66, Sizes).
Overall length	You decide. You can regulate the length with the straps. My top is 32 cm long from the top edge to the top of the ribbed section at the front.

Yarn requirements

One colour	Approx. 3 (4) 5 (6) 7 (8) 9 (10) balls Merino Cotton or Superwash Vital.
ATS	Approx. 3 (4) 5 (6) 7 (8) 9 (10) balls Merino Cotton or Superwash Vital + at least 25 g scrap yarn.
All Over	Approx. 2 (3) 4 (5) 6 (7) 8 (9) balls Merino Cotton or Superwash Vital + at least 100 g scrap yarn.
Bad Idea	Approx. 150 (150) 200 (250) 300 (350) 400 (450) g scrap yarn (p. 260, Yarn Requirements).

Accessories	Stitch holders or auxiliary needles for the straps.
Needles	Circular needle size 3 (60 or 80 cm; for the bottom rib section), circular needle size 4 (60 or 80 cm; for front and back), double-pointed needles size 3 (for the straps).
Tension square	Approx. 22 stitches and 27 rows stocking stitch on size 4 needles = 10 x 10 cm (p. 44, Tension Square). If your tension square is bigger, try thinner needles. If it's smaller, try thicker ones.

A truly cute top, quite easy, but with really nice details. You can also adjust it to fit your chest and waist measurements. The straps are I-cords, which are great fun – an I-cord is a fancy word for a knitted string which is truly easy to make. If you keep pulling the cord downwards while you are knitting it will end up nice and even.

The top looks best if it is close-fitting, not baggy, so measure yourself and choose a size that is very close to your actual size, or possibly slightly smaller. It will also look good if you knit the rib sections and straps with the same yarn or in the same colour. When knitting the front don't forget the BUTT (p. 37).

>

Cross the straps at the back – or not. Whichever you prefer. Bad Idea Scrap technique (p. 110).

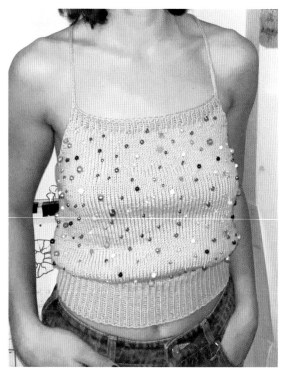

Single colour with beads (p. 244).

ATS (p. 102).

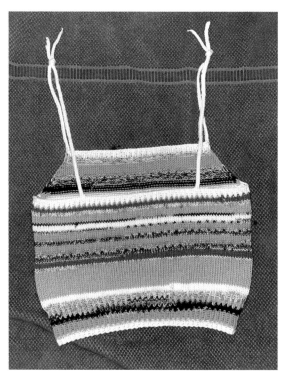

Bad Idea (p. 110).

The Cute Top in Bad Idea Scrap technique (p. 110) with embroidery (p. 186).

Basic pattern
The Cute Top

Front and back

Cast on 142 (158) 174 (190) 206 (222) 238 (254) stitches with circular needle size 3. Join up the stitches to make a circle and mark the beginning of the round = one side of the top. Knit in twisted rib (k1 tbl, p1). In the 1st round, set a marker after 71 (79) 87 (95) 103 (111) 119 (127) stitches = other side of the top. Knit 7 (7) 7 (7) 9 (9) 9 (9) cm in twisted rib. Change to circular needle size 4 and knit in stocking stitch. In the 1st round, increase 20 stitches evenly distributed across the round (p. 61) – 10 stitches on the front and 10 stitches on the back = 162 (178) 194 (210) 226 (242) 258 (274) stitches. Knit in rounds in stocking stitch until your work measures 2 cm less than the desired length from the bottom edge to the armhole. Now knit the rib section at the top of the back as follows: knit in stocking stitch across the 81 (89) 97 (105) 113 (121) 129 (137) stitches for the front as far as the marker. After the marker change to twisted rib on the back (k1 tbl, p1) until you reach the beginning of the round (the 2nd marker). Continue like this for 2 cm, i.e. stocking stitch on the front and twisted rib on the back. Next round: knit in stocking stitch on the front, then cast off all the stitches on the back in rib pattern: k1 above k1 tbl, p1 above p1. Do not cut the yarn. You now have 81 (89) 97 (105) 113 (121) 129 (137) stitches for the front on the needle. Now knit the top section of the top in stocking stitch. Start with the right side of the work facing you and with the right side of the front – that is the side on your right when the knitting is lying flat in front of you.

Knit the BUTT as edge stitch (p. 37), k1, sl1 k1 psso (p. 61), knit to 4 stitches before the end of the row, 1 k2 tog (p. 61), k2. Return row: BUTT as edge stitch, purl to last stitch, k1. Keeping the edge stitches as described, continue with these two rows, decreasing on the plain knitting rows and doing purl on all return rows. Don't forget to BUTT! Carry on until you have 61 (65) 69 (73) 77 (81) 85 (89) stitches or the top is the length you want. Don't forget there will be 2 cm of rib as well. Next row (plain knitting): BUTT as edge stitch, change to twisted rib (k1 tbl, p1) to last stitch, k1. Do not decrease while knitting the rib section. Next row (return row): BUTT as edge stitch, twisted rib pattern (k1 tbl, p1) to last stitch, k1. Continue with the rib section as described until you've knitted 2 cm or the desired length. The next row you should have the right side facing you: knit the first 2 (2) 2 (3) 3 (4) 4 (4) stitches in plain knitting and put them on a stitch holder or auxiliary needle for the straps. Cast off the next stitches in rib pattern k1 above k1 tbl, p1 above p1, until 2 (2) 2 (3) 3 (4) 4 (4) stitches remain. Knit these stitches in plain knitting and put them onto a double-pointed size 3 needle.

Straps

Start with the left front strap = the 2 (2) 2 (3) 3 (4) 4 (4) stitches are on a double-pointed size 3 needle. Knit the stitches in plain knitting, then instead of turning, slide the stitches to the other end of the needle and put the needle in your other hand. Take hold of the yarn from behind your work and knit the 1st stitch in plain knitting. By continuing to knit in the same direction, the stitches will be pulled together to form a tube called an I-cord. Continue until it is approx. 30 (32) 34 (36) 38 (40) 42 (44) cm long or the required length. Cut the yarn leaving a length of approx. 10 cm, thread it through a sewing needle, then insert the needle counter-clockwise through the stitches and pull tight. Knot the end of the yarn several times, pull tight and cut off. Complete the right front strap in the same way. For the back straps: First knit the right strap – the one on your right-hand side when the top is lying flat in front of you with the right side uppermost. Count 18 (20) 22 (23) 25 (26) 28 (30) stitches towards the middle of the work, starting from the right-hand side of the cast-off stitches. Pick up 2 (2) 2 (3) 3 (4) 4 (4) stitches from the cast-off edge by inserting the double-pointed needle size 3 through both loops of the cast-off stitch.

Knit the two back straps in exactly the same way as the front ones, but they will need to be longer, so that the top ends meet. Check by laying the top flat on the table to check the lengths of the front and back straps. They should both be the same length up to the shoulder. After completing the right strap, knit the left strap to match. Darn in or knot the ends (p. 100). Lightly steam the top rib section on the front and back (p. 262). If you like, thread beads onto the end of the straps. Knot the ends so that the beads can't slip off. Knot the straps together, crossing them if you like. *So cute!*

Bad Idea Scrap technique (p. 110) in various colours and sizes. Both tops were steamed lightly (p. 262, Finishing).

𝔅𝔞𝔰𝔦𝔠 𝔭𝔞𝔱𝔱𝔢𝔯𝔫
The Scrappy Socks

You can knit this in one colour or use one of two Scrap techniques.

One colour	Knit with 1 strand basic yarn.
ATS (p. 102)	Knit with 1 strand basic yarn and scrap strands inserted.
Bad Idea (p. 110)	Knit with 1 or 2 strands to achieve the right tension. You will need to knit a tension square (p. 44).
Basic yarn	1 ball sock wool (50 g = 210 m) or similarly thin yarn (p. 263, Yarn Types and Alternatives).
Scrap yarn	Scrap yarn in all colours and shades, but preferably yarns for needle size 2.5 to 3. Shorter or longer strands for ATS. Knotted balls/skeins for All Over. Scrap yarn in all colours and shades for Bad Idea (p. 97, Scrap yarn).
Sizes	36–40 (41–45).
Yarn requirements	
ATS, Bad Idea or one colour	2 balls sock wool or 60–150 g scrap yarn, depending on size.
Accessories	Your mother, aunt or grandmother as moral support.
Needles	Double-pointed needles size 2.5.
Tension square	Approx. 28–30 stitches and 38–40 rows stocking stitch on needles size 2.5 = 10 x 10 cm (p. 44, Tension Square). If your tension square is bigger, try thinner needles. If it's smaller, try thicker ones.

I always say, if you can knit socks, you can knit anything. But don't worry, because the most difficult thing about knitting socks is getting used to knitting with size 2.5 needles. On the plus side, socks are quick to make and a supercool way to use up any leftover odds and ends of wool. I have only listed two sizes because you can measure the length of the sole of your foot and then adjust the length accordingly. I like close-fitting socks best, but socks can always be adjusted to fit your foot. If you have chunky ankles but a shorter feet, knit the larger size and adjust the length to fit your foot. If you have slim ankles, knit the smaller size and adjust that to suit the length of your foot. Measure the length of your foot from the heel to the beginning of your little toe.

The socks are knitted from shaft to toe. I like it when the rib, heel and toe are all in the same wool. You can agonise enough over the colours and patterns for the other parts. Whether you darn the yarn ends in or knot them is a matter of taste – I do both. Lots of knots under the sole of your foot can be pretty annoying, however – so think about that beforehand. You may decide to darn in the yarn ends under the sole or change colours on the top of your foot so you can knot the ends. When I'm knitting socks, I don't limit myself to sock wool, but I do use it for the parts that get the most wear and tear so they last longer. Sock wool contains a bit of nylon, so you don't wear holes in your socks so quickly when you slide across the floor in them. I use double-pointed needles when I knit socks because I don't like knitting them with Magic Loop very much. You can knit the rib section and shaft of a sock as long or short as you like.

>

Single colour with embroidery (p. 186).

ATS (p. 102).

Bad Idea (p. 110).

Socks knitted with the Bad Idea Scrap technique (p. 110). Red and white are always a hit. And Gucci shoes, of course.

Basic pattern
The Scrappy Socks

Shaft

Cast on 56 (64) stitches on double-pointed needles size 2.5. Distribute the stitches evenly on four needles = 14 (16) stitches per needle. Join up the stitches to make a circle and mark the beginning of the round. Knit in twisted rib (k1 tbl, p1, repeat) until you've knitted 4 cm or the required length. Then continue with size 2.5 needles in stocking stitch until the shaft of the sock is the required length. I knit the shaft approx. 9 cm long.

Heel

You knit the heel across the first 12 (16) stitches (on the 1st needle) and the last 12 (16) stitches (on the 4th needle). That means you knit the last 12 (16) stitches of the round on the same needle as the first 12 (16) stitches, so you have 24 (32) stitches on one needle. Slip the remaining 2 stitches from the 1st and 4th needle onto the 2nd and the 3rd needle and put these 32 (32) stitches to one side as you'll not be knitting them at the moment. Now knit a total of 20 (24) rows in stocking stitch. The last row will be a return row (purl). Now you need to knit the heel shaping. On the next row of plain knitting, work the gusset as follows: k13 (17), sl1, k1, psso (p. 61), k1, turn; sl1 purlwise, p3, p2 tog, p1, turn. * sl1 knitwise, knit until 1 stitch before "gap" stitch, sl1 k1 psso (p. 61), k1, turn. Sl 1 purlwise, purl to 1 stitch before the "gap", p2 tog, p1, turn. * Repeat from * until all the stitches on both sides have been used up = 14 (18) stitches. Cut the yarn.

Instep

Divide the stitches from the heel; in other words 7 (9) stitches on each side of the middle = beginning of the new round. Divide them onto two needles = 1st needle and 4th needle of the round. On the two side edges of the heel, pick up 10 (12) stitches from the outer loops on the 1st and 4th needles. Evenly divide the 32 (32) stitches from the instep (which you put to one side) across the 2nd and 3rd needles. Knit one round in stocking stitch across all stitches on the four needles. Next round: Decrease on both sides of the instep (1st and 4th needle): from the beginning of the round, knit in stocking stitch until you reach the two last stitches on the 1st needle, k2 tog (p. 61). Continue in stocking stitch across the next two needles (2nd and 3rd needle), for a total of 32 (32) stitches. K2 tog across the 1st two stitches on the 4th needle (p. 61) and continue in stocking stitch to the end of the round. Repeat the decreases as described on every 3rd round, until you've 56 (64) stitches again. Distribute the stitches evenly – i.e. 14 (16) stitches per needle. Now continue in stocking stitch until the foot is 14 (17) cm long, measured from the top of the heel to the little toe – or knit the correct length for your foot. Try the sock on from time to time if necessary.

Toe shaping

First of all, decrease for the little toe – on the 1st and 2nd needles for the right sock and on the 3rd and 4th needles for the left sock. Work as for the raglan (p. 58). If necessary, set a marker between the two needles.

Right sock

From the beginning of the round, knit in stocking stitch until you have 3 stitches left on the 1st needle and k1, sl1, k1, psso. Now start the 2nd needle with k2 tog, k1, then plain knitting to the end of the round. Now knit a round without decreasing. Knit a total of 3 rounds with decreases in every 2nd round; then decrease in every round until you have 28 (32) stitches left. Slide stitches from the other two needles each time.

Now decrease for the big toe. You do this between the 3rd and 4th needles while continuing to decrease for the little toe as before: knit until 3 stitches are left on the 3rd needle, Sl1, k1, psso, k1, then start the 4th needle with Sl1, k1, psso, k1. Do plain knitting to the end of the round. Decrease on both sides until you've a total of 12 (16) stitches left. Slide all the stitches for the top of the sock (i.e. the stitches on the 2nd and 3rd needle) onto one needle, and all the stitches for the underside of the sock (on the 1st and 4th needle) onto another needle. Thread the yarn through a darning needle and working clockwise, insert the needle through all the stitches, starting with the 1st needle; pull tightly to close the hole. Darn in or knot the end (p. 100).

Left sock

Knit as for the right sock, but as a mirror image – that means that the decreases for the little toe will lie between the 3rd and 4th needle and those for the big toe between the 1st and 2nd needle.

The Scrappy Socks knitted using the Bad Idea Scrap technique (p. 110).

Chapter 10
Crazy Knitting Patterns* (3 patterns)

*Three *crazy* knitting patterns you can't ignore, that no one can ignore when you're wearing them. Just get started. There isn't much more to say. *Carpe diem!* Life is short, so get out there and make the most of it. Learn from your mistakes, forgive yourself and be proud! You deserve the attention!

"The stupidest, maddest, most awesome thing I've ever knitted, and why not to give a damn when people say 'no' and just seize the day instead."

Pleats! I love them! They remind me of the skirts in traditional costumes. And they're supposed to be on trend? Even just the word "pleats" sounds sooo old-fashioned. And that's exactly why I wanted to try them out! Seriously though, pleats are really fun and one of the nicest things you can ever knit. And they're not even that hard to do. Just brace yourself for the incredible number of stitches on your needles. On the other hand, there's only one row or round where you actually have to concentrate on getting the pattern right – which is great!

I started off by making tops with pleats on the sleeves, front and back. To put it mildly, I got completely hooked and started fantasising about being bold and crazy (or stupid?) enough to knit an entire pleated baby-doll dress (p. 31).

So I set to work, drawing lots of sketches with different designs. But somehow I could never pull myself together and get started. It was far too big a project anyway. But when my nomination for the Elle Style Award came in, I finally got going on this crazy project – which actually turned out to be not quite as mad as I'd thought. If you go to a gala, you have to wear gala dress. I didn't have one, and none of the trendy brands wanted to lend me one either. So I had to make one myself. I love a challenge, so it needed to be a project with the potential to go completely wrong. And that so *The Bad Idea Dress* was born. It was really like Cinderella.

The Bad Idea Dress is a gala dress I knitted myself entirely from scrap yarn. It took me 21 days to make – which was exactly how long I had before the awards ceremony. I blogged about it on Instagram, because I knew that the entire project might fail, not get finished, look dreadful or go wrong because 117 other things weren't working out.

I knitted it in garter stitch, which turned out to be an amazing experience – but definitely not one I'd thought through properly. Garter stitch in rounds meant using a circular needle and knitting one round in knit and the next in purl. But that's me to a T: act now, think later. But it's actually an approach I can even recommend. Sometimes. And impossible though it may seem, I did get the dress finished on time. But then the award ceremony was cancelled because of Covid-19!!! And I didn't win either! But you know what? It didn't matter, because the dress was worth it.

I love this dress, because it represents everything that I stand for: not fearing failure or looking stupid, making crazy things that might end up a complete disaster, being open to making mistakes in order to succeed, not worrying about falling flat on your face – or indeed triumphing, believing in yourself, and showing it's okay to be uncertain and vulnerable. We're all vulnerable somehow. And nothing ventured, nothing gained.

The dress isn't perfect, but it's mine. And the reason I'm so happy about it is that it taught me so much about myself. And that's an amazing experience I wouldn't deny anyone. *The Bad Idea Top* (p. 226) is a similar design but less demanding and you can easily extend it into a *Bad Idea Dress* if you're as crazy as I am.

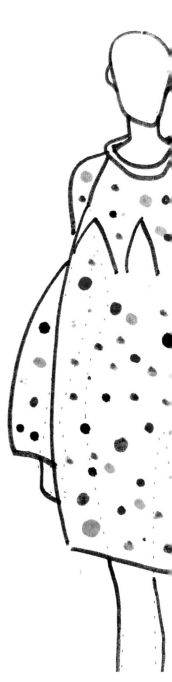

My very first pullover with pleats (p. 222). *Shit*, I was so proud of my navel piercing. I still am!

PRACTISE!

- Before launching in on an entire dress, it might be worth practising pleats a bit first. I've sometimes folded my work the wrong way and only noticed afterwards. I find the folds are the only difficult part, but try it out for yourself. Make a sample with the right number of stitches (if you're doing size 1 (p. 226), that'll be 6 stitches per pleat section). So, cast on 36 stitches and knit approx. 10 cm in stocking stitch. Then follow the step-by-step instructions for a left-facing fold followed by a right-facing fold (p. 224). When you've knitted both the folds, you'll be left with 12 stitches on your needle.

BOX PLEATS

I recommend doing pleats in stocking stitch. I've tried out both stocking stitch and garter stitch, but stocking stitch is definitely the coolest and easiest. To make a box pleat, you place a fold to the left followed another to the right. There are variations, but the principle is basically always the same. Technically speaking, each fold in a pleat has three sections: a front, a middle and a base section. All three need the same number of stitches, and you knit them on double-pointed needles. Knit with the number of stitches given for your size of *The Bad Idea Top* (p. 226). The example below uses the number of the stitches for size 1, which means 18 stitches per fold and 36 stitches in total for the pair of left and right-facing folds that make up a single box pleat.

Left-facing fold in three steps

1   With the right side of your work (the smooth side of stocking stitch) facing you, knit to the place where you want your first fold to start. Slip the next 6 stitches onto a double-pointed needle. These will be the front of the fold.

2   Slip the next 6 stitches onto a 2nd double-pointed needle for the middle section of the fold. Now fold your work so that the front and middle sections are back to back and the two needles lie parallel. At this point, you still have the 6 stitches for the base section on your left-hand needle. Hold this behind your work so the stitches are face to face with those of the middle section. You now have all three needles lying parallel.

3   Now knit the stitches from the three needles together. To do this, insert your right-hand needle through the first stitch of the front, middle and base sections all at the same time. Wind your wool round the needle and slide it through all three loops as you would for a normal plain knit stitch. Make sure none of them slip off their needles! You now have the yarn of the newly knitted stitch on your right-hand needle. Slip the knitted stitches off the needles and pull the thread tight on the right needle. Repeat the process with the remaining 5 stitches on all three needles. You now have a left-facing fold hanging off your right needle.

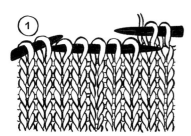
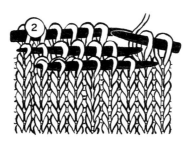
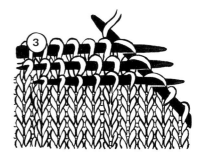

When knitting folds and pleats, make sure you pull the stitches really tight, otherwise you'll end up with a floppy mess. It's also best to knit the round/row with the pleats in basic yarn rather than an effect yarn. But that's a question of taste...

Right-facing fold in three steps

Knit a right-facing pleat in exactly the same way as a left-facing pleat, but in reverse. Here goes:

1 With the right (smooth) side of your work facing you, knit to where you want your first fold to start. Slip the next 6 stitches onto a double-pointed needle. These will be the base of your fold.

2 Slip the next 6 stitches onto a second double-pointed needle for the middle section of the fold. Now fold your work so that the base and middle sections are face to face and the two needles lie parallel. At this point, you still have the 6 stitches for the front section on your left-hand needle. Hold this in front of your work so that the front section of the pleat is lying back to back with the middle section. All three needles are now lying parallel.

3 Now knit the stitches from the three needles together, as for the left-facing pleat. You now have a right-facing pleat.

All in all you have knitted a left-facing pleat followed by a right-facing pleat – which together form a box pleat (an inverted box pleat, to be precise). And it's worked out fine. So, to knit box pleats, simply repeat these two folds alternately until you reach the end of the round/row.

Pattern
The Bad Idea Top

You can knit this in a single colour or use one of the three Scrap techniques.

Single colour	Knit with 2 strands basic yarn.
ATS (p. 102)	Knit with 2 strands basic yarn and inserted scrap strands.
All Over (p. 106)	Knit with 1 strand basic yarn (e.g. Merino Cotton or Superwash Vital) and 1 scrap strand all over (only thin yarns, e.g. Silk Kid Mohair).
Bad Idea (p. 110)	Knit with 1, 2 or 3 strands to get the right tension. You'll need to knit a tension square (p. 44).

Basic yarn	e.g. Merino Cotton or Superwash Vital (50 g = 115m), Silk Kid Mohair (25 g = 210 m) (p. 263, Yarn Types and Alternatives).
Scrap yarn	Shorter or longer strands for ATS. Knotted balls/skeins of thin yarns, e.g. Silk Kid Mohair, for All Over. Scrap yarn in all colours and shades for Bad Idea (p. 97, Scrap Yarn).
Size	1 (2) 3 (4) 5 (6) 7 (8) (p. 66, sizes).
Chest measurement	Approx. 86 (92) 100 (106) 114 (120) 128 (134) cm. Overall chest measurement, measured directly under armholes on knitting (p. 66, Sizes).
Overall length	Approx. 50 (52) 54 (56) 58 (60) 62 (64) cm from shoulder to bottom edge.

Yarn requirements

Single colour	Approx. 9 (10) 11 (12) 12 (13) 14 (15) balls Merino Cotton or Superwash Vital + 5 (5) 6 (6) 7 (7) 8 (8) balls Silk Kid Mohair.
ATS	Approx. 8 (9) 10 (11) 12 (13) 14 (15) balls Merino Cotton or Superwash Vital + 5 (5) 6 (6) 7 (7) 8 (8) balls Silk Kid Mohair + at least 100 g scrap yarn.
All Over	Approx. 8 (9) 10 (11) 12 (13) 14 (15) balls Merino Cotton or Superwash Vital + at least 150 g scrap yarn (thin yarns).
Bad Idea	Approx. 650 (700) 750 (800) 850 (900) 950 (1,000) g scrap yarn (p. 260, Yarn Requirements).

Needles	Circular needle size 6 (80 and 100 cm; for front, back and yoke), double-pointed needles size 6 (for pleats and sleeves, unless you knit with *Magic Loop*), circular needle size 4 (60 and 100 cm; for neckband and bottom edge), double-pointed needles size 4 (for cuffs, unless you knit with *Magic Loop*); crochet hook size 4 (to crochet pieces together).
Tension square	Approx. 14 stitches and 23 rows stocking stitch with size 6 needles = 10 x 10 cm (p. 44, Tension Square). If your tension square is bigger, try thinner needles. If it's smaller, try thicker ones.

This is my favourite design in the whole book. It's easy – but difficult too. Knitting is often a bit of a tightrope act, and that's exactly what I like.

The Bad Idea Dress is inspired by a sort of *ugly* aesthetic and hovers quite definitely on the border of good taste. You'll never tire of looking at the colours and combinations. This dress is incredibly personal and can tell stories of your favourite colours, moods and previous craft projects. If you knit *The Bad Idea Top* or *The Bad Idea Dress*, don't hold back when it comes to colours. Alternatively, limit yourself to just a few shades. You can also work beads in or jazz it up with embroidery. If you do, follow the instructions for single colour and only thread the beads onto the thickest yarn (p. 244). If you're knitting ATS, insert your scrap yarn only into your thick basic yarn. For All Over, use scraps of thin mohair for your All-Over skeins plus a thicker basic yarn as an auxiliary yarn for a nice, more understated look. And yes, you guessed: to turn the *Bad Idea Top* into a *Bad Idea Dress*, just knit the front and back longer. That's all there is to it!

>

Knitted in a single colour with beads (p. 244).

ATS (p. 102).

Bad Idea (p. 110).

Bad Idea (p. 110).

Knitted in a single colour with embroidery (p. 186) and paired with Scrappy Socks (p. 214) in ATS (p. 102).

Basic pattern
The Bad Idea Top

Front and back

Cast on 360 (368) 420 (428) 480 (488) 540 (548) stitches with circular needle size 4 and join up the ends to make a circle. Make sure the stitches aren't twisted around the needle. (Annoying!!). Mark beginning of round with a marker = one side of the top. Purl 180 (184) 210 (214) 240 (244) 270 (274) stitches, set marker for other side, then purl to end of round. For next 7 rounds, alternate between 1 round of plain knit and 1 round of purl. This will produce an edge in garter stitch. This isn't the most fun part of the project, I'm afraid, so just grit your teeth and keep reminding yourself how megacool it will be! End your garter stitch edging with a round of purl. Change to circular needle size 6 and continue in stocking stitch. Revel in the colours, have fun with beads, knit stripes or a single colour. When your work measures 30 (32) 34 (36) 38 (40) 42 (44) cm including the bottom edge (= length for the top), it's time to tackle the box pleats. If you're knitting the dress, continue until it's the length you want and then get ready for the pleats (p. 224). Remember: for sizes 2, 4, 6 and 8 there are two extra stitches on both sides of the markers for the front and the back so the top/dress ends up the right size. Do NOT include these extra stitches in the pleats. Work first left-facing pleat as follows: (Only for sizes 2, 4, 6 and 8: k2, then) slide next 6 (6) 7 (7) 8 (8) 9 (9) stitches (= 1st stitches for sizes 1, 3, 5 and 7) onto a double-pointed size 6 needle. Slide next 6 (6) 7 (7) 8 (8) 9 (9) stitches onto a 2nd double-pointed size 6 needle. Fold work as described on p. 224 and knit the 6 (6) 7 (7) 8 (8) 9 (9) stitches from the two double-pointed needles plus your left-hand needle together in plain knit stitch. Having started with 18 (18) 21 (21) 24 (24) 27 (27) stitches altogether on the three needles, you'll end up with 6 (6) 7 (7) 8 (8) 9 (9) stitches on your right needle when you've knitted the stitches together. You've now knitted your 1st left-facing fold. Time for the 1st right-facing one (p. 225), which is done in the same way but in reverse: slide next 6 (6) 7 (7) 8 (8) 9 (9) stitches onto a double-pointed size 6 needle. Slide next 6 (6) 7 (7) 8 (8) 9 (9) stitches onto a 2nd double-pointed size 6 needle. Fold work as shown on p. 225 and knit the stitches from the three parallel needles together. When you've knitted one left-facing and one right-facing fold plus the 2 stitches for sizes 2, 4, 6 and 8, you'll have 12 (12) 14 (14) 16 (16) 18 (18) stitches for each pleat. Continue knitting a left-facing and then a right-facing fold with same number of stitches as above, until you reach marker for side. For sizes 2, 4, 6 and 8, you'll have two stitches left over before the marker. Knit these and the first 2 stitches after the marker in knit stitch. For sizes 1, 3, 5, 7 just continue alternating between left-facing and right-facing folds until you reach the end of the round. You now have one-third of the original number of stitches left (+ 8 stitches for sizes 2, 4, 6 and 8) = a total of 120 (128) 140 (148) 160 (168) 180 (188) stitches. And that's the difficult bit done! Phew! Now knit 2 rounds in stocking stitch. In 3rd round after box pleats, cast off 5 stitches on either side of markers for armholes = 100 (108) 120 (128) 140 (148) 160 (168) stitches. Cut thread and put work to one side.

Long sleeves

If you're using the Bad Idea technique, check p. 112 for information about knitting sleeves. If not, then just get going. Cast on 30 (32) 34 (36) 38 (40) 42 (44) stitches with double-pointed needles size 4 (or a circular needle and Magic Loop). Join up stitches to make a circle and mark beginning of round. Starting with a round of purl, knit in garter stitch as for back and front – in other words, alternate between 1 round of purl and 1 round of plain knitting. Do this for a total of 19 rounds, ending with a purl round. Change to double-pointed needles size 6 (or circular needle and Magic Loop), mark beginning of round and knit in stocking stitch. In 1st round, increase 10 stitches evenly across round (p. 61) = 40 (42) 44 (46) 48 (50) 52 (54) stitches. Continue in stocking stitch. In 5th round after increase round, increase 1 stitch at beginning and end of round as follows: k2, inc1, continue in plain knitting until 2 stitches before end of round, inc1, k2. Repeat this increase in every 10th row a total of 5 times = 50 (52) 54 (56) 58 (60) 62 (64) stitches. When work measures 44 (44) 46 (46) 46 (46) 48 (48) cm or your chosen length (measured from wrist to armhole, try sleeve on if necessary), cast off 5 stitches on both sides of armhole = 40 (42) 44 (46) 48 (50) 52 (54) stitches. Cut off yarn and put knitting to one side. Knit 2nd sleeve in exactly the same way.

Short sleeves

If you're using the Bad Idea technique, check p. 112 for information about knitting sleeves. Cast on 50 (52) 54 (56) 58 (60) 62 (64) stitches with double-pointed needles size 4 (or a circular needle and Magic Loop, p. 41), join up stitches to make a circle and mark beginning of round. Start with 1 round of purl and knit in garter stitch as for back and front – in other words, alternate between 1 round of purl and 1 round of plain knitting. Knit a total of 7 rounds, finishing with a purl round. Change to double-pointed size 6 needles (or a circular needle and Magic Loop, p. 41) and knit in stocking stitch until work measures 12 cm including garter stitch edging (or the chosen length). Cast off 5 stitches at beginning and end of round = 40 (42) 44 (46) 48 (50) 52 (54) stitches. Cut off yarn and put knitting to one side. Knit 2nd sleeve in exactly the same way.

- You can knit the Bad Idea Top in all sorts of ways. Knitting with so many stitches in a round can be tricky, so be realistic, especially if you choose a Scrap technique. It might be best not to make all the yarn for All Over yourself. A great option is to use mohair as your All Over scrap yarn in places where you can easily knit longer sections in a single colour without spoiling the look (p. 110).

- Because the Bad Idea Top has so many stitches, make sure you check nothing is twisted. It really is the pits if you have to start from scratch because your work is twisted (p. 43, tips for casting on lots of stitches).

Yoke

Transfer all sections onto circular needle size 6, setting sleeves above armholes on back and front. Place a marker between right sleeve and back – i.e. the sleeve to your right when you lay the knitting out flat in front of you with the back uppermost – to mark the start of each round. Re-join yarn and knit 1 round in plain knitting, setting a marker for each transition between different pieces for yoke = a total of 4 markers, including the one at beginning of round. In next row, decrease for raglan: * k1, k2 tog (p. 61), continue in plain knitting until 3 stitches before marker, dec1 (sl1 k1 psso) (p. 61), k1. Slip marker from left-hand to right-hand needle, repeat from * to end of round. Repeat raglan decrease on every 2nd row after that until 40 (42) 44 (46) 48 (50) 52 (54) stitches remain on yoke front. The next round you knit should be a row without decreases. In that round, cast off middle 8 (8) 10 (10) 12 (12) 14 (14) stitches for neck opening, then knit to end of round. Cut off yarn.

Slide all stitches from one needle to the other without knitting them. Now, with right side of work facing you, start the neck opening on left-hand side of knitting – that is, the side on your left when you lay the knitting with the front uppermost flat on the table. Now continue in stocking stitch, in rows rather than rounds.

With right side (= smooth side) of work facing you, cast off for neck opening while continuing to decrease for raglan on plain knit rows. To do this, cast off 3 stitches at beginning of row, knit to end. In next row, cast off 3 stitches at beginning of row, purl to end. In the same way, cast off 2 stitches at beginning of next 2 rows, then cast off 1 stitch at beginning of 2 rows after that. Continue in stocking stitch in rows, with raglan decreases as before on the right (smooth) side of your work until 2 stitches remain before markers on front pieces. With right side of work facing you, cast off all remaining stitches.

Finishing and neckband

Turn work inside out and sew or crochet armholes together (p. 58). Darn in or knot all yarn ends (p. 100). With right side of work facing you, and starting in middle of back, use circular needle size 4 to pick up 9 stitches for every 10 stitches around neck opening. Starting with a purl round, knit a total of 5 rounds in garter stitch by alternating between 1 round of purl and 1 round of plain. On 6th round (plain) cast off evenly and loosely. Darn in or knot ends.

LOOPED-PILE KNITTING

I once knitted a mini-collection of five fur coats and took them to a party. We were all paralytic, and my good friend Peter the photographer took a whole series of photos of us all, blind drunk in knitted furs. To this day, those pictures are some of my absolute favourite photos of my knitted garments.

Looped-pile knitting was developed for annoying design students who enjoy visual uproar and are on a mission to prove that hand-knitting can be more than just plain and purl. I've been knitting looped pile for over ten years, and everything about it is fun – except the vast amounts of yarn it takes. You have been warned! Looped pile is a method for knitting a sort of fur effect. How wild and garish you want your knitting to be is entirely up to you. I used to be crazy about gaudy knitting, but I was still young at the time and felt I had to prove something. Later I began to work scrap yarn into my "furs", one of which became my first proper major sale! I sold a knee-length "fur" coat to a famous artist who gave me some indispensable and unforgettable advice: Start at the top and work down. What she meant was, I should always choose the best shop, the best yarns, the best brand, the best price, the most famous magazine, etc. In short, the best of everything in life. And then work my way down if I was rejected. She also told me not to be afraid of a "no", because it doesn't mean you're not good enough or not the right one, it just means "not now". And there can be lots of reasons for it that have nothing to do with you. Instead, take a "no" as an incentive to try even harder the next time. It's absolutely one of the best pieces of advice I've ever received.

Of course, I've heard ten "nos" for every "yes", but it does make you get your claws out. The crazy freaky fur is indirectly one of the most sensible things I've ever knitted. Contrary to all expectations.

DON'T CUT

To cut or not to cut? I've read lots of instructions for looped-pile patterns that tell you to cut open the loops. I don't, because I'm not sure the loops are firm enough to stay intact. So my official opinion is: *Don't cut!* Let there be loops!

Loops are always knitted with the right side of the work facing you, into every other stitch. Then you just purl on the return row. Looped pile is pretty hard to do quickly, even though it's just one basic stitch. But completing each loop takes a whole series of movements, so it all takes longer. But don't be put off – it's worth the effort.

Looped-pile fur à la Lærke Bagger, 2014 – a bit like The Crazy Loop Fur in the All Over Scrap technique (pattern p. 238).

Looped-pile pattern à la Lærke Bagger in four steps

1   Knit in plain knit stitch until you reach the stitch where you want to make the loop. Knit this stitch too, but leave it on the left-hand needle for the moment.

2   Use the right-hand needle to pull the yarn forwards and loop it round your thumb. This takes a bit of practice, but don't despair – you can do it!

3   Keeping the loop round your thumb, and with the stitch still on the left needle, knit the same stitch again in plain knit stitch and slide it off your left-hand needle. You've now made a kind of sandwich of two stitches knitted into one, with a loop between them.

4   Use the left-hand needle to pull the first stitch over the second to fix the loop. *Voilà*. When you knit the purl row, pull the loops on the front a bit tighter. Very important, otherwise your knitting will end up floppy.

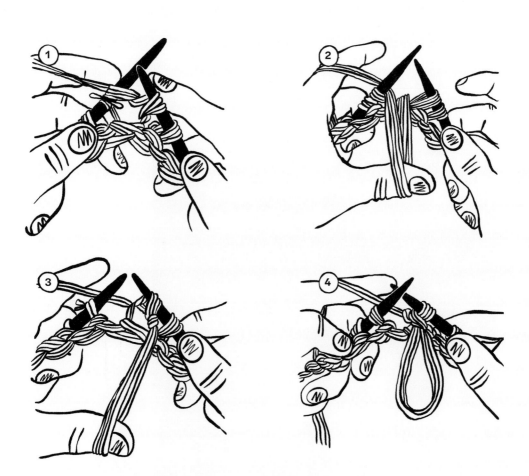

The illustrations show the technique with the yarn held according to the continental method, see p. 24.

laerkebagger

...

Vis indblik   Promover

Synes godt om fra **christinathiemer** og **3.636** andre

laerkebagger SERIOUS BIZ 😎

235

TIPS FOR KNITTING LOOPED PILE

- **Length of the loops:** How long or short to make the loops is entirely up to you. The longer you pull the thread on the front of your work, the longer the loop and the more voluminous your "fur" will be. Make a few tension squares to try out various lengths. Mine are about 8 cm, which is pretty long.

- **Yarn requirements:** This technique gobbles up yarn like no other. You will be amazed how much you need and how heavy your knitting gets. So it's worth thinking about it beforehand and trying out how long the loops should be. It could save you a lot of yarn and maybe a lot of money, if you use expensive yarn. The longer the loops, the more you will spend on yarn. Personally, I love long loops and find the result is worth it. But it's up to you.

- **Number of loops:** You can knit as few or as many loops as you like. In my pattern (p. 238) I recommend knitting a loop into every second stitch. But you can also knit a loop into every stitch. It will gobble up huge amounts of yarn but look supercool!

- **Weight:** Be very careful with heavy yarns such as cotton and bamboo. You'll need a lot in any case, so too heavy a yarn is really not a good idea. An acrylic yarn could be good as an auxiliary yarn as it will make the garment airier and weighs almost nothing. I've been very successful with it.

- **Volume:** The more yarns you knit at the same time, the more volume your "fur" will have.

- **Tension square:** Knit a tension square (p. 44), before you start a looped-pile garment (p. 232). It can be difficult to get the tension right. Tighter is better than loose. Floppy knitting doesn't look good.

- **Pull the loops tight:** While doing the purl row, it's important the keep pulling tight the loops on the right side (the outside) of your work. Do this by pulling at the loop of the stitch you've just purled into. I have a system: I purl 4–6 stitches and then pull the loops to make them longer. Then I purl the next 4–6 stitches and pull the next loops, and so on. It's a slow process, but that's the charm of looped-pile knitting.

On my first "fur" jackets I experimented with lots of different looks. And truly, they still look as wicked as ever!

237

You can make this as
long as you like. Just
knit the back and front
sections to the length
you want.

Pattern
The Crazy Loop Fur

You can knit this in one colour or use one of the three Scrap techniques.

Single colour	Knit with 4 strands basic yarn (3 strands Superwash Vital + 1 strand Inca wool).
ATS (p. 102)	Knit with 4 strands basic yarn (3 strands Superwash Vital + 1 strand Inca wool) and inserted scrap strands.
All Over (p. 106)	Knit with 3 strands basic yarn (2 strands Superwash Vital + 1 strand Inca wool) and 1 scrap yarn All Over.
Bad Idea (p. 110)	Knit with 1, 2 or 3 strands to get the right tension. You'll need to knit a tension square (p. 44).
Basic yarn	e.g. Superwash Vital (50 g = 115-120 m), Inca wool (100 g = 160 m) (p. 263, Yarn Types and Alternatives).
Scrap yarn	Shorter or longer strands for ATS. Knotted balls/skeins for All Over. Scrap yarn in all colours and shades for Bad Idea (p. 97, Scrap Yarn).
Size	1 (2) 3 (4) 5 (6) 7 (8) (p. 66, sizes).
Chest measurement of the garment	Approx. 92 (100) 108 (116) 124 (132) 140 (148) cm. Overall chest measurement measured directly under armholes on knitting (p. 66, Sizes).
Overall length	Approx. 48 (50) 52 (54) 56 (58) 60 (62) cm
Yarn requirements	At least 30 balls Superwash Vital. At least 6 balls Inca wool. At least 500 g scrap yarn. It's absolutely impossible to give a precise estimate of how much you need. Your "fur" jacket will weigh at least 1800 g, possibly more. Read the sections about looped-pile knitting (p. 232) and yarn requirements (p. 260).
Needles	Circular needle size 7 (60 and 100 cm; for fronts, back, sleeves and yoke), circular needle size 6 (60 cm; for neckband), crochet hook size 7 (to crochet pieces together).
Accessories	Buttons, if you want to close the jacket. It looks good with or without.

Tension square   Approx. 10 stitches and 13 rows with 4 strands in looped-pile on size 7 needles = 10 x 10 cm (p. 44, Tension Square). If your tension square is bigger, try thinner needles. If it's smaller, try thicker ones.

This could well be the stupidest and maddest design I have ever made, and that's exactly why I like it so much. Not everything has to be serious or functional. Some things exist purely to cheer us up.

You'll need a huge amount of yarn for this jacket. I've listed the yarn types I know will work well together, but you can get knitting in all kinds of other yarns and colours.

This jacket is knitted in rows in five sections: back, two fronts and two sleeves. Which is good because it weighs such a lot. This is truly not one of your ordinary knitting patterns, and because you decide the length of the loops, it's impossible to provide a realistic estimate of how much yarn you'll need. Also, the amount depends very much on which Scrap technique you're using.

I've listed the amount of yarn I needed, but only as a rough guide. Your needs will depend on the size, loop length and Scrap technique you're doing.

So the best advice I can give you is: you'll definitely need more of what you're knitting with. Also: don't panic.

>

ATS with basic yarn in beige (p. 102).

ATS with basic yarn in white (p. 102).

All Over with basic yarn in black (p. 106).

All Over with basic yarn in blue (p. 106).

I really deserved that beer after my "fur" was finished. Knitted in ATS (p. 102) with basic yarn in white.

Basic pattern
The Crazy Loop Fur

Looped-pile pattern

BUTT 1st stitch, for last stitch k1.

1st row (plain knit with right/smooth side facing): BUTT 1st stitch (edge stitch), *k1, 1 loop in next knit stitch (p.234)*, repeat from * to end of row, last stitch: k1 (edge stitch).

2nd row (return/purl row): BUTT 1st stitch (edge stitch), purl to last stitch, k1 (edge stitch).

3rd row (plain knit row): BUTT 1st stitch (edge stitch), *1 loop (p.234) in next knit stitch, k1 *, repeat from * to end of row, last stitch: k1 (edge stitch).

4th row (return/purl row): BUTT 1st stitch (edge stitch), purl to last stitch, k1 (edge stitch).

Repeat these 4 rows.

Back

Using circular needle size 7, cast on 53 (59) 65 (69) 73 (79) 83 (87) stitches with 4 strands of yarn. Knit in looped pile from 1st row, remembering to BUTT or plain-knit edge stitches at beginning and end of each row. Continue until back measures approx. 30 (32) 34 (36) 38 (40) 42 (44) cm or required length, finishing so that next row will be a 1st pattern row. At beginning of next 2 rows, cast off 3 (3) 4 (4) 4 (5) 5 (5) stitches for armholes. Continue in looped pile, including for stitches you cast off – in other words, knit loop and then cast stitch off so there are no gaps in loops. You now have 47 (53) 57 (61) 65 (69) 73 (77) stitches on your needle. Next row will be 3rd pattern row: continue in pattern with edge stitches, and at same time, on plain knit rows, decrease at each end (without loops) for raglan. Continue to purl return rows with edge stitches as

before. Decrease for raglan on next and all following plain knit rows as follows: BUTT 1st stitch, k1, s1, k1, psso (p. 61), knit in pattern to 4 stitches before end of row, k2 tog, k2 (p. 61) (last stitch is edge stitch). Knit return row in purl. Continue with raglan decreases and looped pile on knit rows, and purl with no decreases on return rows, until 23 (27) 29 (31) 33 (35) 37 (39) stitches remain. On next plain knit row, cast off all stitches in plain knit and pattern – in other words, knit loop where appropriate, then cast stitch off. Put work to one side.

Right front

Using circular needle size 7, cast on 29 (31) 33 (35) 37 (41) 43 (45) stitches with 4 strands of yarn. Knit in looped pile from 1st row on, remembering to BUTT or k1 for edge stitches at beginning and end of row. Knit without shaping until front measures approx. 30 (32) 34 (36) 38 (40) 42 (44) cm or same length as back, finishing so that next row will be a 1st pattern row. Next row: Cast off 3 (3) 4 (4) 4 (5) 5 (5) stitches at beginning of row for armholes. Continue in looped pile, including for stitches that will be cast off – in other words, knit loop before you cast stitch off. You now have 26 (28) 29 (31) 33 (36) 38 (40) stitches on the needle. The next row will be the 3rd pattern row: continue in pattern with edge stitches while decreasing for raglan without loops on armhole side of each plain-knit row. Keep left-hand edge straight, without decreases. Continue to purl return rows with edge stitches as before. On armhole edge only, decrease for raglan as for back: *BUTT 1st stitch, k1, s1, k1, psso (p. 61), knit to end of row in pattern as for back. Knit plain-knit rows by repeating from *. Purl return rows

for back and continue until there are 19 (20) 20 (21) 22 (24) 25 (26) stitches on the needle. Next return (purl) row: Cast off first 4 (4) 4 (4) 5 (5) 5 (5) stitches for neck opening, purl to end of row. On knit rows, continue with raglan decreases on armhole edge of front. On next 3 return (purl) rows, cast off 2 stitches, then 1 stitch on next row, then 1 stitch row after for neck opening. Continue without further decreases at neck edge, but with raglan decreases at armhole edge as before, until 6 (7) 7 (8) 8 (10) 11 (12) stitches remain. On next plain knit row, cast off in pattern so there are no gaps in loops. Put work to one side.

Left front

Knit as for right front, but in reverse – that means do raglan decreases for armhole on left side of front as follows: knit in pattern to 4 stitches before end of row, k2 tog, k2 (p. 61) (last stitch is edge stitch). For armhole, cast off at beginning of purl row. For neck opening, cast off at beginning of plain knit row.

Sleeves

Using circular needle size 7, cast on 39 (41) 45 (47) 49 (53) 55 (59) stitches. Knit looped pile in rows from 1st row, remembering to BUTT or k1 for edge stitches at beginning and end of row. Knit without shaping until sleeve measures 43 cm or required length, finishing so that next row will be a 1st pattern row. Next row: cast off 3 (3) 4 (4) 4 (5) 5 (5) stitches at beginning of next 2 rows for armholes. Continue to knit in looped pile, including when you cast off – in other words, knit loop and then cast stitch off. You now have have 33 (35) 37 (39) 41 (43) 45 (49) stitches on the needle. The next row will be the 3rd pattern row: Continue in pattern

The garter stitch neckband adds to the wild look.

with edge stitches, and at same time, on plain knit rows, decrease at each end (without loops) for raglan. Continue to purl return rows with edge stitches as before. On next and all following plain knit rows, decrease for raglan as follows: BUTT in 1st stitch, k1, sl1, k1, psso (p. 61), knit in pattern to 4 stitches before end of row, k2 tog, k2 (p. 61) (last stitch is edge stitch). Purl return row. Continue raglan decreases on knit rows with looped pile and purl return rows without decreasing, until 9 (9) 9 (9) 9 (9) 9 (11) stitches remain. On next plain knit row cast off all stitches in plain knit and in pattern – in other words, knit loop, then cast stitch off. Put work to one side. Knit 2nd sleeve in same way

Finishing

You now have five pieces: right front, right sleeve, back, left sleeve and left front. Place in a circle on table – front, sleeve, back, sleeve, front – so that raglan edges meet up. Starting at one end and using same yarn as for knitting, crochet raglan edges together in slip stitch on outside of garment (p. 49). Crochet from bottom of armhole to neck opening, inserting crochet hook through outer loops of edge stitches (p. 49). Start all raglan seams from same place. You now have an open circle with a gap between fronts. Crochet side seams between fronts and back together in slip stitch, working on outside of garment. Start one side from bottom and the other from top so seams look the same on both sides.
Now crochet sleeve seams together, working from bottom up on one sleeve and top down on the other. Finally, turn garment inside out and close holes under sleeves in slip stitch (p. 58). Darn in or knot all yarn ends (p. 100).

Neckband

The neckband is knitted in garter stitch, without loops, on a circular needle with edge stitches. With right side of work facing you, use a circular needle size 6 to pick up 9 stitches for every 8 stitches around neck opening. Start on the neck opening of the front that is lying to your left when the jacket is placed with the right side (outside) uppermost in front of you. Knit 4 rows in plain knitting. On 5th row, cast off all stitches. Darn in ends. If you like, crochet round front edges in slip stitch (p. 49). If using, sew on buttons at suitable intervals, e.g. 4 or 5 cm. Congratulate yourself and treat yourself to a piece of cake. You deserve it! Forget about today's gym session – knitting a looped pile fur jacket is just as strenuous as Crossfit.

243

KNITTING WITH BEADS

Try knitting a scrunchie (p. 126) with beads. This is a *Learning by doing* design.

It was knitting with beads that first got people interested in what I spent my time fiddling around with. And it really is fiddly. For my bead designs, you need to be a control freak. They take forever and need a lot of preparation before you can even start knitting. But it's worth it!

Beaded pullovers are the cutest, most impressive, most perfect things I've ever created. I started experimenting with the technique over ten years ago and have steadily got better at it. But the principles are always the same: thread the beads and knit in as many as you like. It's not exactly rocket science!

When I first started with the beads, I could tell something special was happening. It was like an adrenaline rush, like love at first sight. Something magical happens that you can't explain. The feeling got stronger and stronger and a whole new world opened up.

First I did figural patterns. I drew complicated diagrams and made tiny crop tops with lots of looped patterns. One time I got lucky when a celebrity wore one of my tops on prime time TV. I was just breastfeeding my baby when I saw it, and the next morning I awoke to over 100 e-mails from people who'd seen the top on telly. It was totally mad and surreal. The sudden fame of this top made me realise that highs and lows in life are completely out of your control. All you can do is make sure you ride the wave when it comes. And that's what I did, baby at my breast or not, and always following the motto "Carpe diem".

Those crop tops were truly crazy. They looked pretty garish and didn't fit into an ordinary wardrobe in the slightest. They were good for TV, but that was all. That was when I slowly began to give up the showpieces and crazy knitting to head in a direction that would modernise general opinion on hand-knitting and take it to a completely new level.

Gradually, I came to realise there was an easier way of working with beads than drawing and counting until it gave me a nervous breakdown. I'd already developed and used my random principle for scrap yarn and started applying it to beads. I combined different beads in various sizes to create a nice, harmonious balance. The whole thing was a very long and steep learning curve for me, but I like the side of me that the beaded knitting represents: it balances out all the untamed, random, direct, ugly noise of the Scrap techniques – and of myself – with my feminine, sophisticated, romantic side and total love of detail. Beaded knitting reminds me I'm vulnerable and feminine, not just strong, tough or whatever people expect at a given moment. I have all these sides and nuances.

Today beaded knitting has become one of the cornerstones of my designs, which I continue to develop constantly and which I keep coming back to – sometimes after a long gap. Because it's time-consuming, tiring and demanding, and because it's totally annoying but also absolutely fantastic. Oh yes. Important: in beaded knitting, always darn in the ends (p. 65) because it's far too cute for knots.

It's not as difficult as it looks. It just takes a bit longer. If you want to do beaded knitting, it's important to find the right sewing needle for threading up the beads. If possible, use a thin one with a relatively large eye compared to its size. If it's too narrow you won't get the yarn through it, and if it's too wide, you won't get the needle through your smallest beads – and they're important for the overall impression. So look for a suitable needle and take good care of it! Try out a variety of sewing needles, because the thickness of your yarn really does make a difference. The finer the knitting, the smaller the sewing needle you should use.

Thread the needle. If threading a thick strand of yarn through the eye of the needle is difficult, cut a short length of sewing thread – approx. 5 cm – thread it through the needle and knot the ends. Now you have a small loop through the eye of the needle. Put the yarn through the loop and start threading the beads. They'll now slide along the sewing thread first and then along the yarn. Voilà! Clever or what?

How to thread beads

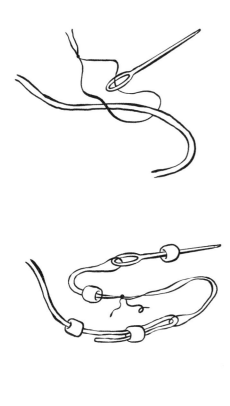

YARN FOR BEADS

- Avoid delicate or brittle yarns like the plague! They tear and get thinner and thinner as you thread more and more beads onto them. Also, if you want to knit in a lot of beads, avoid any yarn that's too heavy – like cotton. Your knitting will get too heavy because of the beads. For the best results, choose a light, relatively smooth yarn.

Knitting with beads in four steps

1 Thread the needle and string together a suitable number of beads, depending on how many you want to include in your knitting. Once you have enough beads on the yarn, remove the needle and push the beads along so you have enough length to knit with.

2 Either cast on with the yarn or incorporate it after the rib section. Keep pushing the beads further along so you always have enough yarn to knit with.

3 When you reach a place where you want a bead, slide the first bead up the yarn and knit it in on your next plain knit stitch. The bead should land on the front of the knitting. Only knit beads into stocking stitch and on the front (outside) of your knitting. Otherwise you'll run into trouble.

4 And now for the most important part: on the next round or row, when you reach the knitted-in bead, knit the stitch through the back loop (pp. 26 and 29). Always. Because that will fix the bead in place. So, if you're doing stocking stitch smooth side out in rounds, do the stitch with the bead as a twisted knit stitch (kbl). If you're doing stocking stitch smooth side out in rows, do a twisted purl stitch (pbl) on the stitch with the bead.

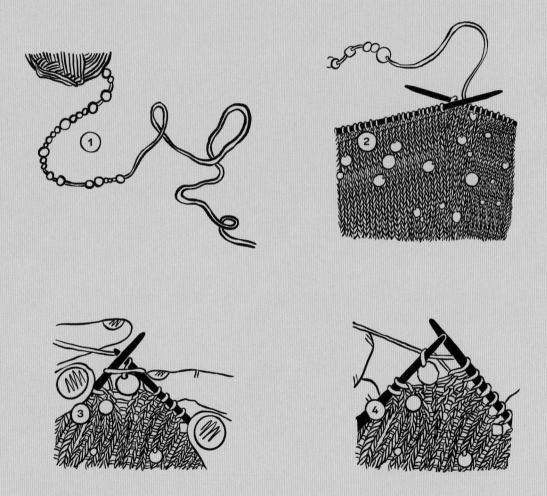

The illustrations show the technique with the yarn held according to the continental method, see p. 24.

Once you've knitted all the beads on your yarn, knit to the next marker (because it always looks nicest if you darn in the ends at the side), cut the yarn, thread a new string of beads and carry on. When you've finished knitting, darn in the ends (p. 65).

How to choose beads

- **Composition:** Choose and combine your beads as you would your scrap yarn to get the right balance and composition. Big words, I know. But it's actually about understanding differences and analysing things a bit. Read the section about scrap yarn again (pp. 102, 106 and 110) and imagine it's about beads instead. Make sure your collection includes glass, wood, ceramic, plastic, expensive, cheap, ugly, pretty, matt and shiny beads. Think in opposites for a more dynamic effect. A basis of black and white beads, for example, can calm things down and balance the many colourful ones.

- **Placement:** How many? How few? Where? You won't find a 100-percent guide as to how to position your beads, because I don't like a sweater to look too balanced or perfect. In a design like the *Carpe Diem Sweater* (p. 252), which has lots of cool details, it's important to make mistakes and for unexpected things to happen. Some of my garments have lots of beads on them, others have fewer. It just depends what you like.

I've been collecting beads for many years, but you don't need so many to make something unique. 100 to 200 g are enough.
<

One of the very first beaded pullovers I ever knitted. OMG did I have terrible backache at the time!
>

IDEAS FOR KNITTING WITH BEADS

- **The right number:** Thread a row of beads onto a length of yarn between 25 and 60 cm. Too many beads on the yarn will be annoying because you'll constantly have to slide them down to knit. But too few beads will mean cutting off the yarn more often to thread on new ones – which in turn means too many yarn ends. You'll need to experiment a bit, so be patient.

- **Start small:** Just knit in a few beads at the beginning. Very few. It's much easier to thread more beads than remove them. When I knit a pullover (p. 252), I only knit 10–12 beads in the first 3 to 4 rounds – sometimes even fewer. That way you can gradually knit more as your work grows longer.

- **The sewing trick:** When you've finished your pullover, you can always sew a few extra beads on in places with too few. That's not cheating, it's just common sense.

- **Children's beads:** I'm wary of so-called children's beads as they tend to look cheap. I don't use Hama beads either, for the same reason. But it depends what you like.

- **Small beads:** The small, annoying beads are the most important ones. They're hard to thread, I know, but they give a garment the exclusive look. If you know how tedious it was to thread them, you understand how much love went into the pullover. They produce a 3-D effect, because they create contrasts and dynamism. So my rule is: if I can get them on the needle, I'll use them.

- **Large beads:** Be very careful with large, heavy beads of glass, ceramic and stone. With time, they'll stretch the stitches and start to hang down. If you're not sure about a bead, get rid of it or secure it by sewing it in with a few extra stitches at the end.

- **Overview:** If it helps, sort your beads into groups of small, medium and large. Use the small ones most frequently, then the medium ones, and the large ones least.

- **Colours:** Work with all colours or limit yourself to one, two or three different shades – as you like.

- **Extravagance:** Invest in 10–20 really, really beautiful beads and make sure you knit them into strategic positions where they'll get noticed – near the neckline, the middle of the front and right at the top of the raglan. That will give your pullover a special touch.

- **Purchasing:** Buy beads in a bead shop, dig out your mother's old ones, get second-hand ones and look out for necklaces with pretty beads and a hideous design, and use the beads for your pullover.

Read through the introductions to ATS (p. 102), All Over (p. 106) and Bad Idea (p. 110) – which are also the principles I use to combine beads for diversity and contrast.

To knit beads into a multi-strand project (like *The Bad Idea Top*, p. 226), thread the beads onto one strand only. Then, use only this single strand to knit the bead into the garment. On the next stitch, carry on with all the strands again. If you knot (twist) a bead stitch with several strands, it will be incredibly tight and difficult to manage.

If you find beadwork hard, awkward or annoying, remember: you just need to get into the flow. Most truly cool things are hard work at first but then they turn out truly awesome.

Best
Your *favourite teacher* Lærke

Pattern
The Carpe Diem Sweater

I always darn in the ends on beaded pullovers, even if there are a lot of them. It would be a shame to knot them on a pullover like this.

You can knit this in one colour or use one of the three Scrap techniques.

Single colour	Knit with 1 strand basic yarn.
ATS (p. 102)	Knit with 1 strand basic yarn and inserted scrap strands.
All Over (p. 106)	Knit stripes with 1 strand basic yarn, followed by stripes with 1 scrap strand all over. Knit all ribbed edges with basic yarn.
Bad Idea (p. 110)	Knit with 1, 2 or 3 strands to get the right tension. You'll need to knit a tension square (p. 44).

Basic yarn	e.g. Extrafine Merino (50 g = 150 m) (p. 263, Yarn Types and Alternatives).

Scrap yarn	Shorter or longer strands for ATS. Knotted balls/skeins for All Over. Scrap yarn in all colours and shades for Bad Idea (p. 97, Scrap Yarn).

Size	1 (2) 3 (4) 5 (6) 7 (8) (p. 66, sizes).

Chest measurement of the garment	Approx. 92 (100) 108 (116) 124 (132) 140 (148) cm. Overall chest measurement, measured directly under armholes on knitting (p.66, Sizes).

Overall length	Approx. 48 (50) 52 (54) 56 (58) 60 (62) cm.

Yarn requirements

Single colour	Approx. 6 (7) 7 (8) 9 (10) 11 (12) balls Extrafine Merino 150.
ATS	Approx. 6 (7) 7 (8) 9 (10) 11 (12) balls Extrafine Merino 150 + at least 50 g scrap yarn.
All Over	Approx. 4 (4) 5 (6) 7 (8) 9 (10) balls Extrafine Merino 150 + at least 250 g scrap yarn.
Bad Idea	Approx. 350 (400) 450 (500) 550 (600) 650 (700) g scrap yarn (p. 260, Yarn Requirements).

Needles	Circular needle size 3.5 (80 cm; for front, back and yoke), double-pointed needles size 3 (for sleeves, unless you knit with *Magic Loop*), circular needle size 3 (60 cm; for rib edging), double-pointed needles size 3.5 (for cuffs, unless you knit with *Magic Loop*), crochet hook size 3 (to crochet pieces together).

Accessories	Beads – if you plan to knit with beads (p. 244), you'll need lots, probably about 100–400 g, depending on the thickness and size of the pullover.

Tension square	24 stitches and 33 rows stocking stitch on size 3.5 needles = 10 x 10 cm (p. 44, Tension Square). If your tension square is a different size, use thicker or thinner needles.

Arrange your yarn, beads and knitting needles on the table and take a deep breath. You're about to take your test of patience and perseverance, and it's going to be a lot of fun.

This pullover is knitted from bottom to top on relatively fine needles, but it's worth the slog. I like using merino wool – it's great for beads and stays looking nice. If you forget to knit some beads in here and there, don't worry. You can just stitch a few more on at the end (p. 250).

As far as colours and yarns are concerned, it's best to choose ones you really like because you're going to be looking at them for a long time. Knit in as many or few beads as you like, and remember: start with a few to try them out. It's better to knit in too few beads than too many. Of course, you could also knit the pullover according to one of the three Scrap techniques and possibly embroider it afterwards (p. 186). It is actually really just a supercool, classic raglan pullover, even though I say it myself. Seize the day and have fun with the design. *Carpe diem.*

>

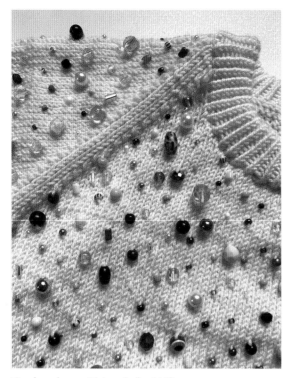

Single colour with beads (p. 244).

Single colour with beads (p. 244).

Bad Idea (p. 110).

Bad Idea (p. 110).

Carpe Diem embroidered (diagram, p. 195). No comment. I love this pullover.

Grundanleitung
The Carpe Diem Sweater

Basic colour white, knitted with beads (p. 244).

Front and back

Using circular needle size 3, cast on 220 (240) 260 (280) 300 (320) 340 (360) stitches. Join up stitches to make a circle and mark beginning of round (= one side of sweater). 1st round: Knit 110 (120) 130 (140) 150 (160) 170 (180) stitches in twisted rib (k1 tbl, p1, repeat), set a marker (= other side of sweater), then continue in twisted rib to end of round. Knit 5 (5) 5 (5) 6 (6) 6 (6) cm in twisted rib, then change to circular needle size 3.5 and continue in stocking stitch. If you're knitting with beads, do the 1st round without beads and maybe start to knit in the beads in the next round. Don't forget: every time you come to a stitch with a bead knitted into it, knit the stitch through the back loop (tbl) (p. 247). Continue knitting in rounds. Also, always cut and change the yarn at the side when your beads are used up. Cut off the yarn and start knitting with a new strand threaded with beads. Whatever happens, don't knot any of the yarn ends as it'll ruin the pullover. Darn in all the yarn ends when you've finished (p. 65). If you're knitting with one of the other techniques, knot the yarn if you like (p. 100). When work measures 28 (30) 32 (34) 36 (38) 40 (42) cm including ribbing, on next round: cast off 5 stitches for armholes on either side of both markers = 200 (220) 240 (260) 280 (300) 320 (340) stitches. Put work on one side.

Sleeves

Using circular needle size 3 (or circular needle and Magic Loop, p. 41), cast on 48 (50) 52 (54) 56 (58) 60 (62) stitches. Join stitches to make a circle and mark beginning of round. Knit 5 cm in twisted rib (k1 tbl, p1, repeat), then at end of round, change to circular needle size 3.5 and continue in stocking stitch. If you're knitting with beads, knit 1st round without beads. Continue in stocking stitch and start to knit in beads during next round. After 1 cm, increase 1 stitch at beginning and end of round (p. 61) as follows: k2, inc1, knit to 2 stitches before end of round, inc1, k2. Repeat these increases every 1.5 cm (a total of 20 times) = 88 (90) 92 (94) 96 (98) 100 (102) stitches. Continue knitting without further increases until your work measures 45 cm or required length, measured from wrist to armhole (Try on the sleeve if necessary). In next 2 rows cast off 5 stitches on either side of markers for the armholes = 78 (80) 82 (84) 86 (88) 90 (92) stitches. Cut off the yarn and put the work to one side. Knit the 2nd sleeve in the same way.

Yoke

Arrange all pieces on a circular needle size 3.5, placing sleeves over armholes on front and back. Set a marker between right sleeve and back – i.e. the sleeve on your right when the knitting is lying on the table with the back facing uppermost = beginning of the round. Join yarn here and continue to knit with beads, scrap or single colour: knit one round in plain knitting, setting a marker for each transition between the different pieces for the yoke = 4 markers including beginning of round. In next round, decrease for raglan as follows: * k1, k2 tog (p. 61), continue in plain knitting until 3 stitches before next marker, dec 1 (sl1 k1 psso) (p. 61), k1*. Slip marker from left-hand needle to right-hand needle, repeat from * to end and repeat on every 2nd row. Don't knit any beads into raglan decreases, as it won't work. Continue to decrease for raglan until 66 (66) 68 (68) 70 (70) 72 (72) stitches remain on front. Now cast off for neck opening, making sure you do so on a round without raglan decreases. Next round: Cast off middle 24 (24) 26 (26) 28 (28) 30 (30) stitches of front section for neck opening, then continue knitting to end of round. Cut off the yarn. Slide all stitches from one needle to the other without knitting them. Now, with the right side of your work facing you, start the neck opening on the left side of the knitting – i.e. the side on your left when you lay the knitting flat on the table with the front uppermost. Continue in stocking stitch, knitting in rows. If you're knitting with beads, remember not to knit beads on purl rows. Also, every time you come to a stitch with a bead knitted into it, knit the stitch through the back loop (tbl). Cast off for neck opening while continuing to knit raglan decreases on front side (the beaded side) of your work. For neck opening, cast off 3 stitches at beginning of next 2 rows as follows: cast off 3 stitches at beginning of row, knit to end – continuing raglan decreases as before. In next row, cast off 3 stitches at beginning of row, then purl to end. On next two rows, cast off 2 stitches at beginning of row, then in next 4 rows cast off 1 stitch at beginning of row. Continue in stocking stitch with raglan decreases on plain knit rows until 2 stitches remain before markers on each side of front. Cast off remaining stitches in plain knitting. Finished at last! Well done! Give yourself a pat on the back!

Finishing and neckband

Turn the garment inside out and crochet or stitch armholes together (p. 58). Darn in all yarn ends if you've knitted with beads (p. 65). Knot yarn ends (p. 100) if you've knitted with scrap yarn. Starting from the middle of the back, with the right side of the work facing you (p. 56), use a circular needle size 3 to pick up 9 stitches for every 10 stitches around the neck opening – in other words, miss out every 10th stitch. Knit 5 cm in twisted rib (k1 tbl, p1, repeat). Cast off loosely. Fold neckband in and crochet or stitch into place. If you've knitted with beads, fill in any gaps with beads. Great job! Take a photo NOW and send it to everyone you know, including me. There's no harm in showing off a little.

Chapter 11
Basic knowledge

"All that boring stuff, which is truly tedious but incredibly important, so read, read, read."

YARN REQUIREMENTS

I must insist you read this, even if it's a drag. This is not a traditional knitting book, because I'm not traditional, and nor are my patterns. Which is why the estimated yarn requirements in the patterns are exactly that: an estimate. A guesstimate, underlined in red. Here are my thoughts and comments on yarn requirements.

There are three Scrap techniques, depending on your personal taste and style, eight different sizes, and the question of tension, which you need to stick to. And there are countless ways of adapting patterns to suit your needs by making them longer or shorter, etc. This means there are far too many unknowns for me to be able to stake my life on how much yarn you will actually need. So use your common sense and cover yourself in one way or another:

- **Purchasing:** When you buy new yarn for a project, choose a shop where you can return anything you don't use. Choose a colour you could use for something else if you have leftovers you can't return. I've always bought more or less yarn without having my sights set on something other than what I was planning to knit immediately. I find it liberating.

- **Colouring:** Check with the wool shop if they have more balls from the same dye lot, in case you need to buy more. Fortunately, for many of my patterns you don't need to worry about the identical shade too much, and if you knit with two or more strands, you'll hardly notice the difference anyway.

- **Scrap yarn:** Save scrap yarn in the same shade, knit with it and keep adding new yarn. Enjoy the differences instead of having a nervous breakdown, and be pleased about the money you've saved. You can spend it on more yarn!

- **Store:** If you've bought too much yarn, add it to your collection. I've never been able to part with any yarn once I've brought it home. Even if it was purple or khaki, which were never my favourite colours. I get attached to my yarns – and I'm probably not the only one! The more different yarns, shades, colours and types I have, the better my knitting is.

In a nutshell: Unfortunately, you'll realise life is not without risk and it's impossible to estimate your yarn requirements accurately if you use scraps.

An alternative "ironing" method. The Nice Slipover, p. 202.

FINISHING PROCESSES AND CARE

Okay, now it's about to get contentious If you happen to be standing, sit down. I really don't rate finishing processes. Really not. I know there are various views on them, but I just use a little steam with only tiny amounts of water and pressure. And only in an emergency. I just don't like flattened fibres much. That's all there is to it. I find most knitting loses a lot of its lively appearance and expressiveness when it's washed or ironed. What I like best is untamed wildness. Of course, I can understand that other people aren't as *freaky* as I am, and so these tips for finishing processes and care are just the ones I like.

Finishing processes and care à la Lærke Bagger

- Don't iron – unless absolutely necessary.

- Don't wash – unless absolutely necessary.

If you can't avoid ironing your knitting, spray a towel with some water and make a sandwich: Towel, knitting, towel. Put some books on top and leave for half a day, or even a whole day. When you use an iron on your knitting, always use an ironing cloth – a damp teatowel or towel. Don't iron the rib sections. Or straps. And don't iron pleats. Nor garter stitch. In short, don't iron anything textured as it will come out flat.

Instead of washing, you can steam knitting with an iron or steamer. It makes the colours more brilliant and can sometimes smooth things out. If you really must wash something – because of wine or Bolognese sauce stains, etc. – then do it by hand in cold water with a suitable detergent, e.g. wool detergent for knitted garments. Treat your knitted garments as if they were whisked egg whites being folded into a soufflé. Okay, I admit it – of course I've never made a soufflé. But be very careful as there's always a risk that your knitting could turn matted or lose its shape.

Dry your knitting by sandwiching it between two dry towels and rolling them up. Change the towels after 24 hours if the knitting isn't dry yet.

Bit of a drag, right? I really can't be bothered, so I never wash my knits. Air them outdoors or take them into the bathroom with you when you have a hot bath. The steam is good for the fibres.

If my little Lars or my big Lulu have been enjoying jam or similar, I just throw the knitted garments in the washing machine (wool programme, 30° C). My life is too short to wash children's clothes by hand.

YARN TYPES

All the yarns I've used in this book are by Hjertegarn, but you can substitute them with other yarns if you can can't find what you want in a particular colour, or if you find wool too scratchy.

If you want to substitute a different yarn type, choose one that has roughly the same run length per 50 or 100 grams, the same tension and is recommended for the same needle size (see yarn information below). Most yarn types are available from the various manufacturers in more or less similar form.

Yarns used in this book

Extrafine Merino 150
100 % Merino wool superwash
50 g = 150 m
Tension approx. 24 stitches on size 2.5–3 mm needles

Incawool
100 % Highland wool
100 g = 160 m
Tension approx. 18 stitches on size 4.5–5 mm needles

Lima
100 % wool
50 g = 100 m
Tension approx. 20 stitches on size 5 mm needles

Merino Cotton
50 % Merino wool superwash, 50 % cotton
50 g = 120 m
Tension approx. 22 stitches on size 3.5–4 mm needles

Naturuld
100 % wool
100 g = 100 m
Tension approx. 14 stitches on size 6–7 mm needles

Silk Kid Mohair
72 % mohair, 28 % silk
25 g = 210 m
Tension approx. 18–23 stitches on size 3–5 mm needles

Vital Superwash
100 % wool superwash
50 g = 115 m
Tension approx. 22 stitches on size 3.5–4 mm needles

ACKNOWLEDGEMENTS

Huge thanks to Hjertegarn for sponsoring the fantastic yarn for this book. Thanks to all my fantastic test knitters – you know who you are. Thank you, Anja and Mette, you're so cool! Thank you, Frederikke, for listening to me droning on and helping me not to lose it entirely. Thank you, Isabel Berglund and Bibi Werner, for believing in a young (and irritating) knitter. Thank you, Evren Tekinoktay, for the best advice I ever received. Thank you, Sune, Lulu and Lars, for putting up with me and for being understanding about all the fuss I made. Thank you, Mama and Bake, for your support! And thank you to Paradisio for the best song in the world, "Bailando", which helps me whenever life is difficult!

Forgotten, what "tbl" means? Need to check up quickly on knitting with beads? You will be glad of these two lists.

ABBREVIATIONS

dec = decrease
inc = increase
k = knit (plain knitting)
p = purl
psso = pass slipped stitch over
sl = slip
tbl = through back loop
tog = together

INDEX